To the Boy
Who Was
Night

To the Boy Who Was Night

POEMS ||| SELECTED AND NEW

RIGOBERTO GONZÁLEZ

FOUR WAY BOOKS
TRIBECA

LIBRARY OF CONGRESS CATALOGING-IN-PUBLICATION DATA
Names: González, Rigoberto, author.
Title: To the boy who was night : poems: selected
and new / Rigoberto González.
Description: New York : Four Way Books, [2023] | Summary: "Rigoberto
González - To the Boy Who Was Night"-- Provided by publisher.
Identifiers: LCCN 2022033104 (print) | LCCN 2022033105 (ebook) |
ISBN 9781954245525 (paperback) | ISBN 9781954245532 (epub)
Subjects: LCGFT: Poetry.
Classification: LCC PS3557.O4695 T6 2023 (print) | LCC PS3557.O4695
(ebook) | DDC 811/.54--dc23/eng/20220721
LC record available at https://lccn.loc.gov/2022033104
LC ebook record available at https://lccn.loc.gov/2022033105

This book is manufactured in the United States of America and printed on acid-free paper.

Four Way Books is a not-for-profit literary press. We are grateful for the assistance
we receive from individual donors, public arts agencies, and private foundations
including the NEA, NEA Cares, Literary Arts Emergency Fund, and the
New York State Council on the Arts, a state agency.

We are a proud member of the Community of Literary Magazines and Presses.

in memory of my beloved mentor

Francisco X. Alarcón (1954-2016)

In xochitl in cuicatl.
Say flower, say song. Say
hello, say goodbye with one
quick breath. Say tahui.
Mi Purépecha se une con
tu Nahuatl: tsïtsïki ka pirekua.
Nimitzilnāmiqui, maestro.

CONTENTS

So Often the Pitcher Goes
to Water until It Breaks
1999

Other Fugitives
and Other Strangers
2006

Black Blossoms
2011

Unpeopled Eden
2013

Our Lady of the Crossword
2015

The Book of Ruin
2019

Dispatches from the Broken World
New Poems

So Often
the Pitcher Goes to Water
until It Breaks

1999

The Flight South
of the Monarch Butterfly

They always return to bring us warmth here in Michoacán
because they remind us of fire: they sputter like candles,
expanding and shrinking their singed browns and reds
as they consume the air in November, finally tapering down

into the shadows like burnt paper. What message
do they carry on their wings from the North—
the place that gave them a brush of black opal
for weight and touches of white to attract the clean

clouds and fool the sun into sending its brightest rays
through the mimic of holes? The butterflies settle their lit
bodies on the naked tree, bringing back its autumn leaves,
those breaths of orange that gasp before falling off again,

this time into the hands of winter. But here, winters
are warm like manzanilla tea. Haven't we always known that,
those of us who chose to stay within arm's length
of our mothers? For some women, sitting like wooden saints

at their doors, these butterflies are calls for blessings
from their sons, the men whose names trickled down to thirst
inside their mothers' mouths. To them, the monarch eggs
complete their prayers like rosary beads, they are the flammable

heads of matches. We value the chrysalis of bone,
the blue shell that brings down the sky within our reach.
By March, when the monarch leaves, a second fever
strikes: the butterflies clusters into wreaths. The trees

the women's sons once owned are set ablaze again; young boys
raise their sticks to cut them down in flames.
We watch together as butterflies drop—explosions bright
as fireworks without sound, yet loud enough to call us out.

The Slaughterhouse

I

Listen.

The slaughterhouse is empty

but you can still hear the squealing—

the echoes, people call them.

These can never leave; they are trapped

inside the walls like stains of blood.

Perhaps,

when the pigs heard their own cries,

they thought they didn't hear their own pain.

All sounds spin inside this house.

They confuse even the pigs.

Pigs don't know when to stop the noise.

II

How strange

that the dogs come near enough

to sniff, but they won't eat the scraps.

They keep their distance, barking

not at the swine but at the men

who hang the carcasses on hooks

like coats.

A pyramid of pig heads

stares out the open door: outside

the men wash off their blood-gloves

in a trough bordered black with flies.
The dogs follow to lick their hands

but stop,
taking their liver-tongues back.
The men's hands still stink of knife blades,
of prongs, and of those fingers
that knot the rope so well. So many
smells. But no one smells the same pig.

III
That's me
standing behind the dead sow.
I'm as tiny as its piglet.
My father took the picture
on my first visit to the house.
I remember it was taller

than church,
but narrow, like an alley.
The intestine strings in the back
didn't look like rosaries then;
they were intestines, running down
to meet the blood pool on the floor.

The sow
looks like she's fencing me off
to the wall, like she has swallowed
half my body. Or is it me
coming out of her pink belly,
born at the moment of her death?

IV

Listen.

The slaughterhouse is quiet now.

The gates have lifted to receive

one eyelid for every eye.

Darkness can be so maternal;

blood spots lip down like baby heads.

Perla at the Mexican Border
Assembly Line of Dolls

Her job was to sort through the eyes
of dolls. Snapping hollow limbs
into plastic torsos had been a soothing task
for Perla, like arranging the peas back into the pod

or picking up spilled grains of salt, one by one.
Since she was born without a womb
and her ears closed up because no infant's shrill
had kept them open, Perla's fingers had developed

sensitivity to dolls: she exchanged
her gentle touch for their rigidity,
which stiffened her bones to the wrists;
at rest, her hands shut down like clamps.

But she could not refuse this trade.
Sometimes she became too easily attached
to the hands, whose curvatures embraced
the crooked joint of her index finger.

She'd go home with her pocket full of arms
too often and would bury them in her garden
in pairs: a right arm with a right arm,
a left with a left—the fingers always pointing

down like roots. After seasons, the only growth
was the ache inside her bones, while her arms
kept shrinking, narrowing like stalks.
Perla asked to be moved to heads.

Here she was appalled by how strands of hair
are jabbed in with pink hooks, how noses and ears
are pinched out, and with what brute force
the mouth hole is ice-picked through.

And for years she had equipped these dolls
with arms too short to massage themselves.
Sometimes she had sent them off
without arms at all, and she imagines

the limbs in her garden digging deeper
into the earth, like split worms madly searching
to comfort their severed halves.
So Perla requested the task of sorting eyes,

eyes that sink into her thumbs
the way rosary beads cave in fingertips.
Yet here she doesn't count or pray;
she only teaches how to dull the pain.

Her gift with a squeeze of her rigid fingers
is the luster of the callused tips,
their stoic gaze. The dolls give up
the sensibility in eyes that do not blink.

The eyes freeze over like the surfaces
of lakes, while Perla's fingers feel again,
though everything she touches slices
clean into her most afflicting nerves.

With the pupil locked in place as if in ice,
each eye stares up accusingly at Perla
as she's about to push it into place: a tack
threatening to thrust back the fury of its nail.

Horn

By the road in Guerrero
a cattle cargo truck stops
at an incline with a flat.

Two brown bulls stand on the bed,
bound by the horns to a yoke—
each captive, hoof-bruised and skinned

at the talus, depending
on his partner for balance.
At the feet, a splash of blood

fiery as a spill of satin,
bubbling down like lava.
A wound burning through the wood?

Not so. The left bull's left horn
broke and flew off the head like
a bottle cap. Defected,

the horn dropped into the brush,
biting through, tip down, making
its first indentation on

its own. Now the bull's skull's left
unplugged like the puckered lip
on a plastic baby made

hollow by an absent thumb.
Stone Anahuac gods have mouths
that empty, that round. This hole's

center is sticky as if
the bull had stuck its black tongue
inside for comfort, the way

we tickle the missing tooth's
gum. Will it grow another?
The bull's left eye, panic-struck,

doubts it, set ablaze with pain.
The head's third socket shocks him
into thick paralysis.

The second bull doesn't move,
contemplating a collapse.
He gazes at his partner—

eye reflecting throbbing eye.
There is no seeking pity,
no screwing the horn back on.

Before the First Man
Stepped on the Moon

On the seventh day
when the seas drew back
and the salt in the pools the seas
left behind had time to seep
into the land, becoming sweet,
the Lord wiped His right hand
and the dust dropped down
on the lakes of Michoacán
to soak up the surface
and bloom into lilies
whose petals smell like the bellies
of the fish.

The truth was
the fish learned
how to smell like lilies, and from them
learned how to rub off their scales
on the sides of the lava stone;
how to stretch their mouths
to suck in the sun; how to gather like petals
and how to disperse,
not with touch but with sound.
And it was here, before the fishermen knew
how to knit a net or unwind a line,
that these fish learned

how to walk on water.
At first it was a sleepwalk, a nightly
balance on the tailfin—a float
over the surface like the unsettled hands
of the drowned reaching up
or like the reflections
of stars not quite settled down,
and it was no miracle.
Nor was this walking forced on them
by the lilies who pushed themselves
closer to shore to make room.
The fish flipped open their gills

and let the moon slip down
their sides and expand underneath them
as if its reflection helped them remain
afloat. So when the first man pushed
a crooked canoe to the center of the lake,
he could not keep from plucking
those wet buoys, those beautiful
fleshed-out lilies as healthy and edible
as the mammal hearts and lungs
he loved to suck dry on land.
The story of the lilies continues:
they had taught the fish

to tempt our hands
to lift them to our teeth.
From that night on, the fish

were to take their deaths
in their mouths to dissolve inside ours.
So important they became we set
a space for them on our plates of clay,
decorated with lilies.
And the lilies took back the lake
unnoticed, incidentally
as the hand
that first dropped them there.

Let it be told, then,
that the fish willed to remain
underwater.
Let it not be confused
with the tragic tale of the snake who
also knew how to walk and who
gambled away that power *and* the ability to speak
when it shared the garden.
The fish knew how to walk
long before any of them; long before
the necessity of safety,
before the necessity

of boats, before the Ark
became necessary; before
man learned to pry open the mouths of fish
and remove gold; before
he learned to multiply fish
as quickly as crumbs from bread; before

he learned how pulling up the nets
to the Lord will unroot
the fish from the lake. Let us not forget
the necessity of fish
or the lessons of the lilies, because
after all that

when the first man took
the first step on the surface of the water,
stepping on the faint reflection of the moon,
if he had only looked back to the lakes
of Michoacán, he would have seen
he was still only imitating fish imitating lilies.

Stars Breaking

We've always been violent toward stars.
As children, stick in hand, we strike
at the piñata in the dark, our cousins guide
near-misses with screams, our mothers
suck in their tongues in fear
that we might club the neighbor's son
and knock him to the hospital again
the way one random swing finding his head
did last year. But not even a bleeding ear
or a bandage the color of crushed plums
could stop us from sharpening
the seven tasseled cones and raising yet another
star up—that plump-bellied sacrifice, waiting
for the rib-shattering blow
that throws its contents
out, heavy heals first. These rewards
are enough to pacify the savages in all of us,
and no skull-cracking or tearing open
of skin as easily as pink tissue-thin paper
can keep the stars from hanging or us
from the inflicted wound and victorious
unhooking. This doesn't keep you up
anymore, Abuelo, bed-ridden, broken-
boned and out-numbered by a riot
of children shrieking like witches on the patio.
Last week you fell off a horse, tonight
that horse goes galloping without you.

Even from that there was a lesson to be learned:
you said we are only mass, becoming
heavier with age, until nothing can endure
the clefts of our wrinkles,
the thickness of our calluses and toes.
Listening to the posada in your sleep,
what, Abuelo, can you make me understand
from that, unafraid to hear a clay
and paper star break open like a peanut
shell between our back teeth? We've
always known those stars are loose
like overcoat buttons, they are elbow scabs,
they're the eye put out by the firecracker, one
of the firecracker's sudden eyes. They're
the glass of the soon-blown fuse,
they're decapitations at the guillotine,
destined long ago to come
tumbling down. Piñata stars teach us
the valuable lesson of defeat,
the lesson of the fall into the dark and how
we each follow that identical path. They show us
not to be disappointed by our loss
of strength or by our separation from
the sky. We are as temporary
as these piñata stars, which masquerade
their mortality with three shades of gold
that like the crowns of your two front teeth,
Abuelo, will glitter to the very end,
until that instant when sound overthrows
light, when the blindfold becomes a permanent one,

and the cries become distant as moons...
or stars—stars because they float above
you, because you don't need to see them
to know they're no longer part of what you are.

Doña María Greets Her Comadre
Doña Luna at the Balcony Window

So you're staying up again, doña Luna, waiting
to guide my sons home from the war.
Then let me help you push out the dark with this face
these hands have wrinkled, a face shaped
the way a restless woman shapes
the folds and furrows on the sheets. How do you
manage it, señora? How do you keep your fingers
from digging into those worries half-stitched

against eyelids? What stops you from throwing down
your cheeks like bowls of beans gone bad, waiting
for the spoon that never comes? What thoughts
swirling within you don't break you off and chisel you?
Someday I too will be bald as rock, having unspooled
the last thread from my head. There is no shame in that.
It's what makes us comadres, a pair of copper cazuelas,
identical molcajetes from the mother stone—

the stone that knows how to hold its breath; the stone
that watches and teaches how to watch; the stone
that keeps the earth in its proper place; the stone
that separates the oceans from the skies; the stone
that stops the floods and snuffs out fires;
that lid of stone, which seals our deaths.
And this old woman will have her peace when her tongue
shatters and all her complaints dissolve into ash.

But you are the unlucky one, aren't you, doña Luna?
Because you will open your eyes a thousand nights
after God has pressed His thumb over my heart
and that night will be the same as the nights before.
And you'll see how one thousand nights after that
worriers and insomniacs still call on you, supplier
of the knitting needle, rocker of the cradle, guardian
of the blue mazorca, keeper of the restless fish.

How everyone looks up to you as if you could solve
the riddles in our dreams, as if you had risen
solely to cut through the darkness of our sleep.
How many times we will expect you to tame bad dreams:
when the child awakens suddenly, with a glint of light
scaring his eye, you'll be asked to help him see within you
the harmless white in a dead hen's tongue,
the Lord's round car, the hand that received his birth.

And this boy will become a man, and that man
might awaken one night to that familiar boyhood fear
and you will soothe him then too, showing him his bride,
her breast, her belly, the wheel that spins inside.
And this man will become an old man, having long since
learned to identity in you his tempered wisdom,
which he will always believe he achieved on his own,
which will trick him into climbing through that hole

and into the pit of the other side.
And another man will rise from the dust,
and another man will unhook his hands from his jaw

to let his voice fly home. And still
nothing puts you out of your sky, nothing—
not the girls who grow their hair beneath you, collecting
secrets like combs and letting in dusks like bedmates;
not the women who round off their faces beneath you,

taking your lines to their calves, your color to their heads;
not the old women who beneath you weave their own shrouds
night after night after night. And every night
is the same night. You were given no choice;
all this time you could have faced the other way
or maybe all this time you never looked our way
and kept us ignorant, because it never mattered that we named
the back of your head "el farol de enamorados,"

expecting you to open a mouth and bring out that passion
called tongue; to lift up the nose like a skirt—
such sweet smells; to expand the cups of the hands,
the pillows of the thighs; to part every cleavage and limb
and expose the hidden moistures caught between dark
and light. How much does it matter if you ever tried
to show us different, when we'll always believe
it is you sending lust through our veins? You're to blame

though when we jerk our heads like owls, trapped in the woods
by the noises of night, you give us your quilt
and say nothing. When we show you the sores on our feet,
those tears on our skins like old clothes,
you give us stitches and expect nothing.
So what comes next? Do we lift our empty hands and mouths

in your direction, and will you, kind señora, good
mother, take nothing in exchange for your bread?
Poor doña Luna, poor comadre, there is no rest for you.

We have given you so much responsibility, that we've forgotten
what tiny bones we have, what small spaces we occupy.
Today, here we are: comadres, a pair of curandera eggs
sucking up the cries that keep the alleys wide.
Tomorrow, my body may adjust itself under the sheet
and you'll wait up for other sons alone, señora. That's why
I'm here now, weak and sleepless, pretending this night
I'll pluck one burden off your eye.

Walking by the Panteón San Franciscano

NOTICE

Effective fifty years after the date of your death,

those of you who don't pay perpetuity will be uprooted.

For more information, please walk over

to the civil registry. Ask for Chela.

In this cemetery, you can buy perpetuity

with pesos. For only fifty, you can keep

the mossy hair you'll never learn to comb,

the fingernails you'll forget to stick inside your mouth

for comfort, though even if you remember,

your fingers will slip out just after the lips

slide in. You can have the shroud that will eat

through your skin after you've split the seams

on your sleeping shirt. But you'll own every button

on that shirt and every bead on your rosary bead and every ring.

And though the beads and the stones won't wake anymore,

you can be sure they're safe, collecting at the bottom

of your coffin. And your teeth, oh yes, those teeth

in the back of your mouth, the ones you never used

or saw, even those will finally be yours to keep.

But you'll also keep more valuable things, like your cross,

yes, you can even keep your cross—

that gold-plated cross your godparents wrapped around

your catechism or the all-gold one your mother gave up
when you married in the church she and your father married in.
Whichever one you end up with, you will keep.

Isn't that what you, a good Catholic, will want to do?
You'll crease each finger over the knuckles, both
knuckles over the chest, and then the ribs will cave in

over the lump of dust which used to be your heart.
And you'll fold over and over again until you are
layers of thin tissue, pious as a Bible.

Don't be fooled if your cross seems to have grown:
you have tried to shrink down to the size of your cross.
You have tried to be devout and hinge yourself on it

like a miniature Christ. And that will be
your own little secret blasphemy to keep in a box
and tuck away the way you used to store

old love letters, the way you will store your own tongue.
This you will learn and this knowledge too
you will keep. And no one will take that

or anything else away from you. No one
will ever search inside your pockets or disturb
the way you pile up your ash or tip your skull.

For only fifty pesos, you can keep all those things
you took with you—the few belongings even God
won't rattle in His collection plate.

Mortician's Secrets

1.

The most of righteous part of the body
is the armpit with its delicate growth of hair.
The armpit has withheld more gossip. It has kept quiet
more than our privates, complacent
in a corner that when exposed we choose to ignore.
That's how it became so respected:
it took advantage of our faces turned sideways, our embarrassed
looks, and then imitated that humility.

2.

Mouths always spit out their final sentences.
Until then the jaws remain locked as if biting down
on that last word: the location of the car keys, a cry
for help, the name of the face the dying recognized and thought
they could pronounce before closing shut. The dead
sometimes do this purposely—an attempt
at grasping the world they feared to leave behind; at holding
on to a memento, which could comfort them when pressed
slightly against the tongue. Sometimes it is
accidental that word is there at all, having been
abandoned or compressed within the throat at the moment
of death. Either way, the mouth eventually lets go.
That word turned solid as a marble or a broken tooth
surrenders to the quietest of hours.
The word squeezes through the lips and reclaims
its ascension back to sound when it bounces

off the chin: a bead of sweat melting on the griddle—
a blue kiss coming up for air.

3.
A woman's ash tastes
different from a man's. Remember how as children
we shook the sawdust off old church floorboards
with our weight? While on our knees we
reached down to draw obscene figures, then licked
our fingers clean. A man's ash will remind us
of the days we missed those pictures with the Host;
of catechism days when we spread the orange
coating of bricks to affect a bloody tongue
during silent prayer. A man's ash tastes of old pinole, of common
dust—bedroom dust sucked up excitedly
within the fury of sheets.

But a woman's ash is not as easily
compared. I can't explain it with anything
I've tasted, but certainly with elements I've never dared
to touch. Taking her ash was like
discovering the outlines of the woman's fingers in the glove,
of the head beneath the hair. It was finally knowing
the taste of sugarcane pulp a woman discreetly
spits inside her napkin. It was digging out the thin
crust of dirt between her toes and around the curve of her heel.
It is something not quite forbidden or
inaccessible. It is the flavor of what could have been
and which I savor even more because it wasn't.

4.

Before the bodies leave the parlor, I dress them
in my coat. Not my black mortician's coat with its heavy
scent of lily stems and tarnish, but my blue one, the one
I haven't worn myself. It's not a body in my coat
that excites me, but rather that of my
fleshed-out coat inside a coffin,
its collar and shoulders pushed out against the lining as if
with the weight of the coat's deep color and not of
the corpse. In my coat the body vanishes. The face becomes
an afterimage. The gold buttons show through
the crossed hands. I'm persuading my burial coat
to be selfish, to want its own space, to keep itself company.
I'm teaching it to be its own body,
and like the body insist on reshaping the edges
of the coat on its own and on demanding
to twist and bend all objects of the parlor
toward itself. Already the lapel rejects
flowers whose petals don't fade
into blue. When I die I will dress my death in that coat
and allow my absence to become the main attraction.

What Smells Dead

If through whisper and caress we sense them,
if the yellow light sneaking out
at the splitting of their bones betrays them,
why not notice the dead through smell?

Grandfathers, those smokers,
are subtle, dismissing an aroma of breath
penetrated by the lit match
or of that final suck—the faint burning up
of the filter's edge
as if in quiet protest for having been buried

in clean coats. Old women take
their old women smells and insist
on keeping them clasped
to their clothes like spare bobby pins;
but their graves will radiate like warm glass,
the air made heavy—
the odor of burnt sugar escaping the pot.

The dead don't always have idle smells,
like those that linger at the tips
of gloves or those that rise from the mouths of shoes,
from the chair just emptied;

there is also the discharge of passions.
In lovers, the older the corpse, the stronger the letting go.
Secrets finally surface;

the skin submits to its own decay.
Hands set free their collection of sticky oils;
necks and thighs give up the touch
of other hands, the scent of money;
tongues release their love of liquor, of tongues.

The rest are also gluttons: they smell of basil
and cloves. Their bodies exhume the spices
that in death consume the flesh.

Yet frequently, the dead remain unnoticed—
we believe they no longer smell like us.
At night, these smells don't wake us,
but we still absorb them, then breathe them out.
Through us,
they settle on the moss like sweat.

Taking Possession

I'll begin with the simple things:
your extra comb, your sock, learning to trace
a strand of brown hair until I darken it,
exhaust it between my fingers;
learning to fill in the shape of your foot

with my fist. I'll do this every night for a week.
When I'm ready, I'll slide the comb back onto the crowded dresser
and replace the sock where you last left it,
taking up space behind the hamper. Then I'll claim
the indigo button on your favorite purple shirt and the bookmark

keeping page 130 from
131. These I will not return as quickly, not until
I master slipping the button on my tongue,
trapping it against the roof of my mouth like candy,
which will never surrender its sugar. But it's not a flavor

I crave, but the image of your shirt, opened
at the sternum, exposing that dividing line, which ends
on your upper belly. Perhaps you'll never wear
that shirt again. Perhaps it will hang in the closet,
completely unbuttoned. Then it will all be mine.

The bookmark I'll remove to make you lose
your place in *Cien años de soledad,*
though when you find page 130, 131

will be missing. I'll finish it for you, out loud.
I'll stand before the mirror, imitating the tones

you make when you say "Tú," when you utter
"Sí." And once I too own the gift of shrinking
the lips into a knot, enclosing them to a perfect *o*,
we can read the rest of that page together: you
mouthing the syllable, me reflecting it. I'll practice

breathing out the way you do when you write
and when you sleep, a sound so slight, so soothing
it must not have come from the nose, but from a stranger
source. I'll mimic this strangeness until not even I
can detect my listening.

And while you're gone, threatening never to return,
I'll learn from your soap
how to conform my hands and feet to the nooks
on your body; from the pillow, I'll lift the creases
the right side of your neck has left behind.

Your couch will teach me all about positions;
the light switch will coach me on the craft of unbending
angles into lines. And when I learn to open the door
the way you do, knowing exactly what you'll find,
I'll enter, burdening the carpet with your weight,

smelling of afternoon sweat, damp cotton, and glazed skin—
brown like yours. I'll fool this chair, this bed,

and especially these walls when I approach them
with your heat. I'll keep your possessions
perceptive, greeting you through me.

So Often the Pitcher Goes to Water until It Breaks

a poem in four voices

1.

You know they say, manita,

so often the pitcher goes to water,

so often the man reaches in

to tickle, to probe, to run his finger

across your leg the way the designs

move slowly around the water pitcher, disappearing

long enough to tease and coming back in time

to find their place so smoothly

that your eye fills in the gaps.

And as night leaks into day,

this man will wash his hand

in the lake before going home, thinking his wife

will never trace those dirty fingernails

to the oils in your sweat.

And what will you have then?

A thumbprint etched against your thigh

as visible as a smear on the pitcher's clay.

2.

It's not because of his longest fingers,

not their crawling out, searching for an itch,

not their settling on the knee, docile

and moist as a dog's nose. It's not because of his knuckle

or its five hard nipples. And it's not his wrist,

that cool tongue. Those arms, smooth thighs, are not

why I let him submerge his body into mine.
It's his resurfacing, when he
closes his arms, tucks in his wrist, covers
his knuckles, withdraws his fingers,
taking part of me with him the way the pitcher
takes away its drink from the lake—discreet enough
to make the villagers think it is still intact.
It's when he emerges and goes home with me in his belly
that I learn to occupy his salts.
Those hollow body prints he left behind? I'm
filling them up with myself, making myself
expand. I am
                    stretching, I am
                              getting larger
Soon I will be all oceans, deep stomachs,
and when I swallow him next, I won't want to spit him back.

3.

The secret is in their curves, compadre, women
are all roundness—hips, buttocks, breasts,
elbows, knees, shoulder blades—it's all
in the way you collect them, how you
take each ring and slide it on your finger,
how you begin with the smallest circle
and make it the heart of a bigger one, which in turn
is the heart of a bigger one, just like the ripples
in the lake, with so many centers that no matter which
you pull out of the water, it is absolutely the heart
of something. Of course, compadre, you cannot call them
circles, or rings, and it would not be wise to tell them

that there are so many of them. Tell her
she's the only one. Tell her she is the reflection of the moon,
but don't tell her that means there are two
of them then, and that she is the second one,
or that moon has her own reflection at the lake
already, or that anyone can take
that reflection home in their water pitcher,
or that anyone can drink the moon that night
and expel it by the following morning.
Don't tell her, compadre, that even the moon
has curves, and that those curves, like any other
curves, can possess a touch or a look
but can never control the hand or own the eye.

4.
Only so much will I pretend this rete-cabrón
kept his hands in his pockets all day, fingers
folded down like a puppy's ears.
Only so much will I believe he kept his prick
tail-limp and tame between his thighs, thighs
so weak, they're as quick to spread apart
as a mouth opening long before the tongue wants out.
I don't need to sniff his hands
to know they've been digging up
new smells; I don't need to touch his feet
to know the toes have been dipped in a stranger's
sheets. It's all in the way he walks in
through the door—tilted, half-tipped
like a pitcher, having just given itself
out. He thinks there's plenty of himself to pour,

poor thing. Soon he'll have emptied out

completely, and he'll be easier to crack,

weightless shell. And how much

of himself will he carry then? What part of him

won't leak and sink through the floor?

You know what they say:

So often the pitcher goes to water—

Tanto va el cántaro al agua—

So often the pitcher goes to water

until it breaks.

Other Fugitives
and Other Strangers

2006

Other Victims

Thank heavens for victims who find their way
to folly. They walk on the lean streets in your place
and into a world rich with abuses. Their fates would have
no place to shine if not for that journey, the possible
headlines, the sigh pushed out by the odd relief that

it wasn't you. You are lucky. The man you live with
would never kill you, not in the violent way
other people die—all horror-flick theatrics with costumes
so dirty they could only thrive in other parts of town,
not here in the quiet rooms where your only surprise

is a kiss from behind. If he ever wanted to be rid of you,
your lover would do it kindly: perhaps a poison that falls in love
with your sleep. A compassionate man, he won't let you die
in public, or alone. He won't let you suffer
without him. Never worry. He'll take care of you at home.

The Blue Boy Next Door (and His Lover)

after *Zephyrus* (2002), a painting by Tino Rodriguez

For the wayward angel any bird's wings will do—
the pheasant's, certainly, because it flowers in the hunt.
Or perhaps its distant cousin's, the peacock, coquettish
in his courtship frock. In any case your body craves

attention. Your fingers are aflame from tearing the teal
sheets on those nights your lover leaves you. You cry
into the whiteness of your hands until they're pink enough
to make the bedroom glow and wake the neighbors.

If you press your palm prints to the window's glass
will the neighbors pity the pair of starlings smoldering
across the street? If you bind the creatures by the necks
will they cease their shrieking? Drama queen, every

blue inch of you screams for a wound. It's the only way
to secure your man's return. When he comes he's yellow
with famine and will need to sink his teeth into your flesh.
He has already eaten out your heart and can never kill you

that way again. But you want him nonetheless; no other
mouth knows the fierce pulse of your blood. And none
can match your stare, so heavy you bruise when you blink.
And what do the neighbors think when you toss a kiss

and it strikes the wall like rock? Let them listen in.
Your lover's at the door, the show will soon begin. Once more
you play the injured prey and he the eager predator
whose hunger quickens with the smell of easy game.

Crooked Man

He owns a crooked tongue
that jams his grief inside his crooked mouth
and no one hears the news that
I have died.

Neighbors say I'm still inside
his crooked house, which, when I entered
months ago was not a dark cocoon of wood
and bone. I should have known

better, people will declare when
I'm finally extracted like a nail.
But until then I'm not mistaken in
the kinder things I've learned

about this man who wants to change his crooked, crooked
ways. He apologizes when he strikes, he
craves forgiveness. When I drop it
on his tongue he savors it—

coaxes out the peppermint
to soothe my wounds. No touch
can heal the way his does, starving pain away
with promises. No promises can hold more hollow bowls.

Only Bluebeard's wives have grown
so wise, seeking out forbidden rooms

because they want to wear the secret of their lover's
lust—passion so dangerous it's fatal.

This man I love will never tell
his side of it. He mourns in silence.
If only he could sing my ecstasy—imprisonment
within his crooked, crooked heart.

Rapist: A Romance

The quarter shone on his palm like light entering a hole in the bone. If fear had color his hand would have bruised. I wanted to place the tip of my nipple on the icy metal just to understand him a little more. Instead I took the coin and watched his body float backwards as if I had lifted its last anchor. He waved goodbye. The last speech in his mouth spilled out the way I had made him give up his words many times: thickly and slowly and red.

*

Our first night together I watched him sleep so peacefully I could have slit his throat. I held the tip of the knife inside his nostril, his ear, his navel; he might have itched in his dream. I let him live through the night and I knew he would leave me some day. The next morning I kissed his eyes through the lenses of his glasses. I disappeared behind the smudges. It was useless to see me coming.

*

I called him Pretty Cock because it was so perfect when it stiffened into carved bone. The skin of his head matched the nipples matched the anus and I realized what a simple confection he was. I confirmed it by what small imagination he displayed when he left and came back to me, wearing the same socks, speaking the same basic vocabulary of *love* and *yes* and *no* and *please.*

*

He was irresistible in that white terry cloth robe that curtained the hairy hamstrings of his legs as he bent over to check the bath. He was irresistible in the wet sleet letting go of its clear coins on the black bathroom tile. He was irresistible slumped across the bathtub with the dark algae of his hair opening and closing on the surface of the water. Fucking him while he almost drowned—that was irresistible.

*

He told me how when he was twelve his mother had killed herself while he watched from the door as she took pill after pill as if in a trance. I told him how when I was fourteen my father had watched me do sit ups in the living room until the night he pulled my legs over his shoulders and made me shit on his cock. He told me he had tried to kill himself the same way his mother had. I told him I didn't have a choice either.

*

Amor, I miss pressing my tongue to your pulse as I clench your wrists between my teeth. I miss the discovery of your heartbeat as I bite your neck. You said we fucked like cats and that night you clawed your way out from under me and made me chase you to the balcony. I pressed against you on the railing. I miss your back magnet-sticky on my chest like that. I could have pierced you perfectly so that my head slid painlessly through your moon's silver ring. But I missed.

*

I saw him waiting for the bus one afternoon. The black coat made him look like a piece of iron balanced on the curb. I wanted to push it forward to flatten on the street with the heavy clang of metal vibrating through every vein of concrete. But I wasn't letting go that easily. Not yet. Not with that quarter still burning a hole in my stomach since the last time he left. He said to call him once I got over my fist-to-jaw reflex and I swallowed the coin just to spite him.

Other Fugitives
and Other Strangers

The nightclub's neon light glows red with anxiety
as I wait on the turning lane. Cars blur past,
their headlights white as charcoal.
I trust each driver not to swerve. I trust each stranger
not to kill me and let me cross
the shadow of his smoky path.
Trust is all I have for patrons at the bar:
one man offers me a line, one man buys the kamikaze,
another drinks it. Yet another wraps his arm
around my waist. I trust him not to harm my body
as much as he expects his body to remain unharmed.
One man asks me to the dance floor, one asks me
to a second drink, another asks me home.
I dance, I drink, I follow.
I can trust a man without clothes.
Naked he conceals no weapons, no threat
but the blood in his erection. His bed unfamiliar,
only temporarily. Pillows without loyalty
absorb the weight of any man, betray
the scent of the men who came before.
I trust a stranger's tongue to tell me
nothing valuable. It makes no promises
of truth or lies, it doesn't swear commitments.
The stranger's hands take their time exploring.
Undisguised, they do not turn to claws or pretend
artistic skill to draw configurations on my flesh. They

are only human hands with fingertips
unsentimental with discoveries, without nostalgia
for what they leave behind. I trust this stranger
not to stay inside me once he enters me.
I trust him to release me from the blame
of pleasure. The pain I exit with no greater
than the loneliness that takes me to the bar.
He says good night, I give him back
those words, taking nothing with me that is his.
The front door shuts behind me, the gravel
driveway ushers me away. The rearview mirror
loses sight of threshold, house, sidewalk, street.
Driving by the nightclub I pass a car
impatient on the turning lane. My hands are cold
and itch to swerve the wheel, to brand
his fender with the fury of my headlights.
But I let this stranger live
to struggle through the heat and sweat
of false affections, anonymous and
borrowed like the glass washed of my prints
to hold another patron's drink.

Good Boy

Wasn't I a good boy once? Wasn't I
once stripped of body hair and knuckle, a laugh
so clean it stretched like a white sheet on the clothesline?
Wasn't my voice once
the contagious note of a two-finger bell?

The rust in my throat now coats those high-pitched sounds.
If there is a child in me, he hides
behind the dull flint of my hip. Not alive,
not dead, but lost in the stomach
to dissolve like any other

color. Old photographs don't persuade me
that I could have grown into a man
who could love other men with self-restraint,
who would not ask a man to sleep
on the sharp blades of the bed

without complaints. Surely my anger had
always been squatting on its claws, eager
to tear its way out of my ten-year-old ribs.
Then how do you explain this
strange ability to inflict pain?

I must have ingested hatred
through the spoons of my childhood.
I must have been the changeling matured

now longing for things that blister
and boil. Whatever you place in my hand

I want to puncture out
of mischief. Or perhaps the intentional act
of uncoiling comfort is to get
at its irritated heart and confirm that
even the purest odor stings.

Lover, when I drive the nails into your chest
your mouth opens, white
and pasty like a moon. Do you
see me waving back twenty years ago
from the distant planets of my eyes?

Papi Love

If Papi stops loving me, I'll look for a man who acts
like a man, who opens his brown heart like
a wallet in public places, who burns slowly as a
cigarette in bed, who is unafraid to intoxicate
with his ash—a brave man, thick-nostriled, scarred,
whose only unused muscle is his inhibition. Show me

a man who can't hold back from plunging his fingers
into his lover's flesh and you've shown me a man
who licks his hands clean of my sweat and
blood. I want to stay so pure, so elemental, so
mattered—a property essential as air
that practices its warm seductions in the lung.

Give me a man who describes my every crease and mole and
knuckle, and I have a man who can cradle my entire
body in his mouth. I need that god, that judge, that
father who hugs me like the son he never wanted
to give up, who wants me back inside his womb, unborn,
undressed across the sheets that helped conceive me

A man made me a man and only a man
can hurt me, unlocking my lips from the copper
nub of his nipple, withholding the milky
dish of his hand from my thirst. A selfish man
becomes barren and chokes on his own white dust.
A man generous as a church is going to be

my man, my give-it-to-me-till-it-doesn't-hurt
Papi, sideburns graying to an overcast sky, groin flash-
ing with lightning, hairy chin that tickles down my back
like rain. Ask me who loves me and I'll tell you
who I am: I am the keystone held intact by the arc
of his arms, I am the texture that exists at the command of

his touch, the scent of pressed carnations dead
until it comes alive beneath his nose. I am
that shadow of a man. It's because he steps into the sun
that I am. It's because he breathes that I have
breath. It's because I wake up in the morning
with the wide clock of my face still beautiful

and ticking that I know I'm worth a man.
If Papi stops loving me he can't be that man
and I'll kick the tired animals of his hands
off my path. If Papi stops loving me he never was
a man. Without me he'll never be a man because I am
what makes a man a man.

Vanquishing Act

Disrupting symmetry: the key
to the art of conquering

a lover. Take exactitude and
distort its vain

proportions. Cover the navel: de-
center the belly; hide

one nipple: lose half
the torso; conceal

the sex beneath the cold
knuckle: disorient the groin. Fitting

substitute: mouth.
Swallow ear, chin, nose. Tug

appendages like Picasso's
canvas. Like a wet brush

stroke them flat. Say
minus. Say cancellation.

Negate one leg,
wedge your foot between

the ankles, divide
knees. Lock the limbs into a

landscape of
irregularity. Splinter shadow,

dent bone.
Variation: plunge the face,

tongue—that
practiced breacher—

into the river of thighs.
Claim all other estuaries:

tear elbow from
rib, split buttocks, dig deep

into the root of armpits,
anus, throat—

thrust them inside
out. Bandage the missing skin

with yours. Fill up the craters
in the flesh. Graft hair.

Make him so much you
only you can make him.

Complete dominion:
unlock the shoulders,

snap the clavicle,
collapse the spine.

The pelvic bone folds
inward, the foreskin back.

Femur slips inside tibia
like a pipe. Press down

firmly. Muscle pleats.
Say fraction, say rhomboid

suitcase—magician's box
that opens at the jaw.

Inside, the heart keeps pumping
like an anxious rabbit.

Danza Macabre

Your wreath declares: *I celebrate my coffin because it keeps me*
longer than my mother. Wood polished to patience as the tantrum
of your body wastes no time to soften. As your grudges forgive
themselves, as your indiscretions uproot from their hiding places
to crawl away like larvae, as the stones of your gossip tumble off

your tongue, you're gratified somehow that all your flaws
and all your crimes will be absolved. That's what you believed
into the final hour, and found comfort in that fantasy while I
nailed my doubts to my skull and said nothing. Now the soil tightens
its grip on your coffin and my thoughts take wing: if what you said

were true, lover, cemeteries would be the cheeriest homes
with their laughter six feet deep and a nursery of cherubs
blowing at the pinwheels on the Catholic stones. And somewhere
behind the water tank would wait the caretaker in his cardinal
frock ready to pounce with confetti. What a treat to frolic

with the dead and their souls climb like carnival balloons,
music from the organ grinder driving the monkey to madness.
How fortunate the deceased like you, stiff-fingered, lock-jawed,
unburdening your bodies without effort, the seven sinful sisters
settling to clear the murky water of your blood. Even the fiery

mood of your eyes cools off like lava, and you appear human
again. Perhaps even humane. Death is so tolerant and forgiving
even with those who were not. You can take your make-believe

afterlife with you. I am alive, and the breathing can allow for other
theories. In my cosmos of karma, the dead swim like fetuses

in their personal purgatories and must drown their way out
of their earthly deeds. The scratch and bruise come back
to roost in the hand that fathered them. The bark and scream return,
clotting the throat until it implodes. Even the prodigal kick leaps
up to the bone, demanding to be sheltered again in the quick-tempered

spring of the knee. Past offenses multiply the memory cells of the flesh,
bubbling the brain into oblivion. That is how I see you now: fury coma
self-consumed into spasms. Wouldn't it be nice for the victimized?
I suppose however that neither you nor I will be humored, that the end
has surprised you as much as it will me when the sky closes up

like the fist we've both seen as often as night. At long last, when my body
also dims to gray, we'll be equals, companion corpses, gracefully
retired like a pair of ballet slippers, predator indistinguishable from
prey. Let the rosaries murmur that lovers make peace in their graves.
Let the sun search for spectral kisses. Let the moon bless the padlock

as the living leave and shut the gate. No fugitives permitted here—only
debts and those who resolve them. Goodbye, my former love, be
patient as my body marvels at the world without you. In a year or decade
I'll be dead and we'll converse again through all eternity. Partnered in
our favorite dance, your phantom holler with my ghostly screech.

Body, Anti-Body

I'm lifeless because lifeless
gifts are what my partner gives
me: words that gnash without teeth,
limp orchids masked as kisses,
the sexless fuck of neglect.

His lust became wallpaper-
tame after only a year
in his bed. His mouth forgot
how to suck and gnaw and lock
itself around those tender nubs

that please me. Displeased, my flesh
began to seek those strangers
generous with touch. With them
I'm not a name, I'm body,
I'm not a ghost, I'm living skin

that craves the skirmish scars
of passion and taking stock
in the dark of nick and bite
and bruise, the stench of triumph
thickening air. These men act

on instinct, with violence
that drives and thrusts and imposes
pure punishment upon me.

I love my sudden lovers
anonymous and loutish.

I know I'm alive when I
mend with stitches, when my heart
hammers against its lonely
cell, grunt and groan companions
in delightful exertion.

Oh, the temporary itch
of fingertip and tongue. I'm
as famished as the street
devouring all sensation
at any point two people

meet. Wink and I'll respond. Smile,
I'll exist. Detachment drops
me dead into the sinkhole
of my partner's sleep. Therein
my curse: to be the sweetheart

fierce with sweat, to taper down
to thinning bone and shrinking
marrow, to mad shriek without
throat, to palpable shadow
drilling its nose to the wall.

The Strangers Who Find Me in the Woods
after Thomas James

The strangers in the woods must mimic squirrels and crackle
with the undergrowth. They must not flinch at the cruelty
of breaking golden leaves with their feet, or of interring stones.
And like any of these deciduous trees in autumn they must be

stingy with shadow and move deceptively across the sludge.
I listen to these strangers stirring with the evenings. I invent paths
for them to the soft edge of the lake. Each descent is as graceful
as a sinking ship, but less tragic somehow because these strangers

don't possess a lung. I cannot hear them breathe, yet the air
is all whispers, all sighs—the same ethereal muscle that rubs
the color off the foliage. I lost my way out of the woods on the night
every bird went south or numb. A plump rat snatched the moon

and dragged it by the white rope of its tail. The strangers were
a cloak of silhouettes flattening against a trunk like bark.
I must have disappeared among them because the mouth I touched
was not my own and was cruelly closing in on someone's rib. I carried

such a bite on me, an arc of green and yellow on my side from the man
who said he loved me. In that darkness I knew as much about him
as I did of the amputee swimming his way up the hill with his
only arm. So this is the home of the unturned stone where

the fugitive keeps his kiss? Archeologists will find a paradise
in the place no touch died of neglect. Is it any wonder all things
forgotten or abandoned find their way here? The winter is back, so too
the bloated body of a book I tossed over the bridge last week.

And there on the bench, is my old smoking habit, a cigarette
glowing on my mouth like a beacon. I'm patient, waiting for the fugitive
to claim me as his own. I'm as wise as any stranger here, alone but with
the knowledge that the grief of separation is always brief.

In Praise of the Mouth

Your throat, moan-cluttered, opens
like the desert's flower. The tongue quivering with thirst
is not the stamen, but the wet union of exposed
corolla and nocturnal bat—the sharp sting
of pink, the accidental fang of red. With me inside,
your mouth transforms into a pair of leeches
fattening sucker to sucker, an
uroboros swallowing its glutinous reflection
to retrieve a slick coat as it spits itself back.
Neck against neck, two voices dance
through the madness of the Venus's flytrap, the rattle
in the hinges of its blade is not
death, but the cry of love—what the narcissistic
moon hums to the sea that mirrors it.
Even the alligator's dangerous parade of teeth
looks beautiful because it celebrates the mouth.
With or without the ringing uvula of welcomes
your cave still softens into silk
when something finds its refuge there. And there
stone shatters, undressed of blue crystals,
bone melts to marrow, and hearts implode,
shriveling down to the plum pit origins of lust.

Skin Preserves Us

Pick another body. Any
body. All bodies recognize
similar functions.

If you move
it learns
to move with you:

its foot imitates
your foot; its nipples stiffen
to mimic yours;

the thumb, that absent-
minded wanderer, eventually
matches your thumb.

Pick a body: limb
by limb, bone
by bone—one tooth

at a time,
screwing each molar,
each incisor,

into your own white gums.
Don't be hasty
selecting a tongue—

sample enough of them
to make a wise decision.
Sample plenty since

tongues tend to be
fastidious, unlike
the gullible anus or seductive

cock, both easy
to please. Fat hearts
adapt as quickly as elbows

and knees. Everything is
interchangeable. Entire
bodies, replaceable.

Including yours.
The body you wear now became
sick from overuse.

Your lover
simply left, leaving you
temporarily untouchable

with a body
thick with bruises,
thin-skinned to near-

transparency.
Before you disappear
completely, pick another

body, another mouth,
another pair of hands, softer
than the ones that used to

hurt you. Pick out
another face, but careful
with the eyes.

Snap each one
into your hollow
sockets, make sure

they'll hold
down the lonely
dawns with you.

Black Blossoms

2011

Floriuno

Orquídeas

Your life began this way, with the dream of orchids, bone-white, gristle-
like, pollinated by flies. Then again, life ends this way as well: with flowers,

the smallest regrettable sacrifice. In the dream, you are not the orchid,
or the fly, you are the shadow in the flower's funnel—the line of darkness

that withdraws into itself like the crab pulling its exoskeleton back. A fly
laps at the petal with its needle-tongue. That is not death but the knowledge

of death, the prosaic detail an important one eventually. Then what is death?
The orchids themselves? The dream? Neither. The orchids are simply orchids,

the beauty and the grief of life. Every flower that blooms implodes: aromas
are the legacy of ghosts. The dream is voice finding its throat. Have you ever

seen sound? The whiteness of the orchids, the fly, the shadow draining down
to the shaft—all of this is sound. Did it not travel to your mother's bed

and into the fever of your sleep? And the dream—it means the fear of exiting
the womb and of entering mortality. Arrival means death.

Floricuatro

Baby's Breath

Every birthday you eat a year off your mother's life—your mother plucked
in parts, petal by petal like the disappearing daisy, stares down as her heart

bubbles out vulnerable as yolk. The needle-thin rays of the sun
press against her every morning when she opens her mouth to yawn

and exposes the waking weevil of her tongue. What is it about mothers
that makes them so mortal? Is it that every mother bleeds? Is it that every

mother weeps into the jaundiced rags of her hands after the bodies she hums
into the world exclude her? Yes, you'll leave her, first memory of your gums.

She slumps among the furniture and marvels at the temporary power
of populating houses. Skin and wood, these are the archives of her hours.

The floor maps footsteps with cracks on the tile. Your mother records
the sounds of her sleepless nights. This is what keeps her alive

for now: the sleepwalk through the walls as she lactates through her robe,
your baby's breath settling like the snowdrift in a dusty water globe.

Floriséis

Sleeping Murders

Illusion of sleep where the dead forget to keep still. The poppies
of their eyes take to the light and melt like crayons. Palette skulls.

You dip a finger in your grandmother's socket and paint
the scarlet back into her cheeks. Invent a name for this resurrection:

floreo. Minutes from now your awakening will murder every
flower in your head and you'll be none the wiser. Your great-

grandmother was an exquisite gardener and when she died her tulips
burst like swallows on the wire following the report of the gun. Dumb

birds, dozing with moth-cramped gullets, the down drifting off into
another dream. Bisabuela, magician before her death: give her a mirror

and she'll multiply parakeets in the cage, give her a flea-ridden dog
and she'll extract from a mutt an exotic Dalmatian. Give her a girl

who sleeps inside the coffins of her foremothers and she'll plant
perennials near the crib to teach her how to bring back the dead.

Black Blossoms

after Goya, Madrid

Sisters, with your grinning skulls hovering
   above the gutted stomachs of your bowls,
your teeth look so pretty when you pray.
   Say the word *broth*, say the word *mutton*

and the kitchen mocks you with dust.
   Even the cupboards have picked the teacups
clean. Say *famine* and the black magic
   of the word rewards you with resolved

conflict: dead now the old debate over poultry
   or fish—the chicken coop wireless,
the lake a sand trap that swallowed the dog.
   When the dog refused to yap at its dark

luck you tittered at its only act of bravery:
   the deliberate leap into the mud.
Poor desperate bitch, teats like beads of hardened
   wax, the dandelion of its head

jutting out in spite of its wish to forget the pity
   of you mummified mistresses,
the wooden spoons in your hands the reachable
   crucifix you split between you.

You might have eaten the dog, but it had
        three legs and you none, your femurs
long-since tapered to the floor. You stare each other
        down and laugh, consuming

the only edible resignation: humor. What is
        misery now that the last spring
you will ever know has already been forgotten?
        What is pain when the final blister

has been bitten off and broken down?
        Old widows, with your backs to the windows
you won't need light outside of your widow gowns.
        When the sun sets next it will

blossom with the blackest mushrooms and the moths
        will lay their eggs on your leathery
smiles—oh wicked wicked larvae bubbling in protein
        much too late. Isn't it funny how

whatever moves from this minute forward sets
        itself into motion without muscle?
Your hollow throats chuckle as your dimples
        digest their cheeks, as your tongues

deflate with your thighs and breasts, and as your
        bodies spasm at the last chance
for sensation: the pucker and stretch in the sutured
        centers of your gray vaginas.

Mise-en-scène

after Lizzie Borden

You are not a woman,
          you are not a ghost,
or the shrill that makes the neighbor's hounds abort.

You are not a space between buildings,
          not wind tunnel or porthole
through which the indigent cat slips in and out of its coma.

You aren't the hermetic door with its back to the street,
          you are not the echo to the cracking wood,
or the footfalls mimicking distance

as they spiral down to the dark hole of a center.
          You are not the center.
You are not the interruption of the window

surprising the postman as he skips the tin mailbox once more.
          Every person in this house has died.
You buried your mother with a plum pit in her throat,

you buried your father without his hair or his shoes,
          you buried the hair inside the shoes.
The shoes behave like flowerpots and wait for the moss to grow.

What does a creature do
          in the tar pits of its own extinction
but lift its tusks to the heavens to pierce its own wail?

You are no less dead than the parakeet
        that gnaws at the chips of paint.
Father said to keep it in its cage

but you want something else to die before you
        hand over the room to your corpse
and disintegrate like the stack

of Father's pornographic magazines in the fireplace.
        You are not the immolation,
you are not the woman pressing her shriek to the page.

But you know about turning black, limb by limb,
        You know about finding a smile
on the mantle and detached from its skull.

You buried your father without his teeth.
        You buried your father the night
he wanted to step inside you the way he enters the house.

You are not the dress
        that opens from the outside like an iron gate,
you're not the stupid woman

with her finger shoved inside her mouth.
        When she goes up in flames
she will melt into the fruit bowl.

You are not the fire, you are not the bowl.
        You are not the reason the parakeet
sputters down to the floor in a trail of smoke.

This is not your bird and this is not your house.
        You are not the screeching sirens.
No, you are not the owner—

he disappeared into the mattress and left his bones.
        You're not the daughter,
you're not the spouse.

She's in the kitchen.
        She can't get out.
You're not the poison in the soup,

you're not the knife or gun or noose.
        You're not at home.
This is not your burning house.

The Girl with No Hands

after the Brothers Grimm

Your father asked for more than a polka-dot tie,
      a self-portrait in Crayola
or cinnamon snickerdoodles flat as candle stubs

on the baking sheet. He grabbed you
      by the wrists and severed your hands
to wear on his key chain like a pair

of lucky rabbit's feet. What's so
      fortunate about a rabbit hopping
about the prairie with a missing limb?

What if all four of its legs had been clipped?
      It eats only as far as it can stretch
its neck, and then rolls itself on its back

to perforate its starved belly with the blades
      of its ribs. When the hunter returns,
the rabbit will have its revenge, looking like

the amputated foot of his diabetic mother
      wearing that familiar bunny slipper.
Your father seized your hands, not out

of malice, but greed—his wish to match
        Midas and pocket the small golds of his
kingdom—Rolex, wedding bands, crucifix,

and the precious treasures of your rings, which,
        little princess, will never leave
your fingers because Papi breaks no promises.

He never abandoned you either,
        always there when you see the hairbrush,
perched on the bristles like a nesting pecker.

Resolute, you age with ingenuity, learning to eat
        right off the branch, nibbling apple, apricot,
and pear without separating fruit

from stem. This is how you heard about
        the clever rabbit, from the hunter's son
who made love to you pressing his fists

to the small of your back. He locked you
        against the tree trunk and your shoulders
splintered the bark. What a miracle

of an instrument, the piano that's played
        with elbows and knees and four clumsy
heels that for all their random reaching make

the sweetest rhythms. Your bodies
        danced each afternoon in the grove
while your mother sewed the mysterious

tears in your dresses. You forgave your mother's
            inactivity that night when Papi struck
down your wrists with a cleaver, the mirror

of the metal like a window to a furnace,
            the shadow puppet butterfly emancipated
finally. Who knew chopped bone could sing?

Maybe a chicken doesn't utter a note at its
            beheading because its mother
hen isn't near to cluck a frenzied requiem.

Your mother squealed as fiercely as a
            sow and your stumps looked like the bloodied
snouts of swine. But all that rage escapes

you now as you unleash the power of the hand
            your father left intact, and with it grip
your lover tighter into you. So this

is delectable defiance, Miss Rabbit—
            it must have been a female to claim
the last word. You, girl with no hands,

can produce another pair and more:
            legs, torso, head, and a bear trap of a jaw
to bite the hands that feed her.

The Beauty of Guanajuato

A woman knows her husband's secret pleasures. My father's
were slips. When I saw him through the keyhole, swinging

his hips like a hula girl I couldn't wait to tell my mother.
And then I saw her foot tapping out a rhythm from the bed.

I wondered how they had reached that moment, he
confessing his passion for silk stretched across his bare crotch,

she indulging him since his penis had fattened like the clock's
weight when he hiked up the skirt just before sex. That night

flickers like a reel of film especially now in my own
bedroom, with my own husband neglecting to touch me again.

How to coax him into speaking his desire? Like this: lifting
his lip as he sleeps, I uncover the need that presses his tongue

against his teeth. Oh stealthy detective, I know that scent
of rigid earth that flies out when he whistles. So I shadow him

to the underground museum, the mummies posing like
department store mannequins. He stands for hours like the dead

reflection of the dead woman in a velvet dress. She, a true
Catrina with her gums receding to affect a smile. Her fingertips

soiled as if she had dug herself out of the ground. What amuses him?
The hands that he can snap in half like crackers, the leathery flesh

that he can peel back as easily as a tangerine's, or the sunken
eye pits staring out like assholes? I must admit she's quite a beauty,

this dead thing that poses like a lady, her spine braced with pride.
The left toe pokes out like the nose of a mouse and I feel the urge

to kiss it. My husband must be wishing the same since once
he craved the accidental gift of my wrist exposed between

coat sleeve and glove. This dame is full of secret blessings·
a missing button at the top of her blouse reveals the unbridled

ends of thread; the opened collar provides a glimpse of the valley
of the delicate neck; and in the neck itself grows the root-like

architecture of wrinkles and bone. I step into the light,
approach my husband from behind and join him on the glass.

We, now a threesome stacked in a communal grave, encased in an orgy
of short breaths. I place my hand on his shoulder. He splits

my fingers with his thumb. The dumb corpse grins with complicity
as if she knows, oh yes, she knows, that she has joined this

couple in their bed. Husband runs his knee to lift her dress.
Wife invites the bristly skin to rub and rub against her skin.

The Ballad of Lucila la Luciérnaga

Tijuana-Mexicali, Baja California

Mine is a familiar tale: I ran away with the circus.
When the trapeze artist swung from platform to platform,
a hole in the tent his elusive halo, I knew the devil's

mischief was at work and I had no choice
but to leave my bedridden father without filling
his water pitcher or emptying the bedpan or singing his lullaby

the way I always said I would should the prince
in his storybook tights leap out of the pages and into
the humid afternoons of a border town so dark with people, one

more moribund shadow makes no news. Headlines come
from this: a circus caravan plunging into the gulf of La Rumorosa—
canyon steep as the depths of the imaginations

that immortalized the ghosts there. Vehicles collect
at the pit like the discarded shells of uncooked shrimp.
When the elephant trunks drop limp among the chimps

cracked opened like coconuts, the mad poet fits the oddly-
shaped cadavers into the lines of my song. Lucila la Luciérnaga,
young girls will weep at my tragedy and never leave

their fathers lest they risk my fate—whinnying for all
eternity's midnights like the orphaned fillies found roaming

among the rubble for phantoms. Could I defend myself

I'd say that splattering into the four directions was just
more places to go. *Only joking, girls.* My humor was
the first gift of my freedom, reclaiming laughter my father

took from me each time he beat me when he couldn't beat
his wife. When my mother died, I knew my day would
come to seek a life, and found it with circus folk who understand

the romance of stallion courtship, the elegance of lions licking
at their furry knuckles after mating. To make love among
the beasts is to lie across the dreamscape of animal passion,

where every whimper, every grunt finds a body and creates
motion. My lover called me *firefly* by the way my buttocks
lit up at the height of excitement as he took me from behind.

I wore a skirt with lights after that, guiding the horses
with a wand around the ring. Lucila la Luciérnaga, the audience
called me, and my lover winked from the highwire.

As the circus wagons rolled down the canyon, no different
from cages suddenly, my lover placed his hand on my ass,
a complicit touch that said this was the fall without a net,

exactly as he dreamed it nights before when he awoke
to the groan of the bear giving birth. He reached over to insert
his fingers in me as he said: *Lucila, baby, please turn off the light.*

Thinking Stones
Seattle

She said stones are capable of thought. They had to be:
any object with sound could think. Something about

the waves trapped inside of rock, memory of time.
Something about rock's metallic viscera. The Japanese

had it right, cultivating a contemplation garden on a bed
of sand fluid as blood, each rock electric as a brain, she said.

Dementia brought out the poet in my mother.
I sit at her side writing down what intrigues her: horses,

because they wear a fifth hoof over the mouth; flashlights,
because they can't keep secrets; and stones.

Lately, even the gravel has been buzzing with collective
thought: death, the last mystery to what has crushed

all else beneath its weight. My mother pities that,
and comforts a stone in one hand. I remember

my own soft fist inside her fingers years ago, when
my mother could roller skate and guide me

through the shaky sidewalk. When she laughed, I imagined
doves in flight, seed puffs escaping through the fence,

and everything else that ascends toward light. My mother
doesn't keep her days of wonder, nights of anguish anymore.

I think fossil, I think watermark, about the stubborn
barnacle that makes a tomb of its home. The woman

next to me is the place of my birth and will free me
to wander the shifting plates of the planet on my own.

She can leave without me, deaf to my cries, my pleas,
my fear of getting locked out of her house. I must stand

before the apathetic widows. No use knocking on the door,
I think sleeping oyster, think coma, think stone.

Vespertine

for Roxana Rivera

Stop-breath, stop-time, stop-world, steering wheel.
            Those who don't drive solo don't know
about the only lane a day from midnight on a road so lonely
            it considers transit company.

The zero of the hour darkens tunnel-socket
            right behind the car and always the winking
cyclical theater of the path just ahead. The bloodshot mirrors
            hypnotize and never a question

about how tree shadows operate without the puppeteer.
            Though suddenly nothing has strings
attached—not the croupy voice rattling the dashboard,
            not the pedal pushing anvil-foot,

not the fingers tap-tapping a devil's tattoo.
            Even the watchdog moon, so bored with the old
story of a single unit forcing light to the eye-stinging minutes
            of yawn, unhinges its coat

and hops off its stool. Without the moon,
            the night has turned its black. Without the moon,
the moth flattens its crêpe against the windshield
            to rub its prayers against glass. What parade

this? A word on a young woman's tongue, a word
            at her fingertips, a word inside her ear.
But if she's alone was there ever language? Simple mercies
            love silence though the engine

has its own sordid tale, a once-upon-a-sight,
            a happily-never-after, all device and no plot.
Scratch that, cancel that, back track—
            the young woman's mind reverses the jump-start:

gas up and begin again.
            Stop-breath, stop-time, stop-world, steering wheel.
Those who don't drive solo don't know
            about the sensuality of midnight, coy as an evening gown,

as a plunging neckline, as gloves
            that seduce the arms to the elbows. Knees apart
on the vinyl seat and a voyeuristic mirror
            waiting for the naked lips to dance beneath its oils.

And suddenly everything has beauty mark
            status—the windshield night-bathing its chest
of white freckles, the hood pushing forth
            the trophy of its traffic scar, the smoky skirt

sprouting diaphanous blossoms in lieu of the spill
            of a dirty martini. Even the bristly moon,
in dire need of a thorough exfoliation, unhooks
            its bathrobe and heads for the spa. What flights

of fancy this? Cassiopeia sending her five-spoked

        vanity from above? Without the moon to out-shout her,

she can call to the pretty girls below. Without the pretty girls

        the country thickens like the gulfweed

over the Sargasso Sea.

        Road where the dead end snakes through the dark

with its stomach stretched, won't let the buoy

        catch in its throat. A room off stage is waiting

for dirction; all of its corners costumed

        in kohl. But what if the actress never shows?

Does the production close? The cloud rafters

        unfurl into complaint and the cardinals bubble like blisters

when they hear their moan. Ladies

        and woodsmen, drop your violets, asters

and toothworts on the prairie floor. And the wolf

        will not startle and the moon will keep its O.

And the daybreak will evaporate its sorrow.

        And hunters will aim for the elk and watch

the curves of its flanks erase themselves

        from the canvas striped with autumn oak. And the breeze

will caress the meadow as if the ripple

        of sound has nowhere else to go. How fortunate

the thinking wishful that they can instruct

        a landscape of prose that rises to the roof and never tumbles—

not even when it shatters its hip.
      This is the part where the young woman enters.
This is the part where she leaves. Her life
      so quick it could have been missed had she left

no evidence for the blackbird to construct
      its nest. Collector of pity things, what synecdoche
makes your chickadees mourn to chirp?
      Tweets the beak: a fiber bending like a Mississippi estuary,

memory of a blouse a woman wore
      to dance with her beloved father...when sun
the warmth of pacific waters, when wind
      the chime of México. When dusk

the ghost of a thousand feathers of winter migrations now
      unborn. Exquisite exhale, spiral of snuff
that drills its point into requiem. Rosary seeds
      too trapped in pit to ever split. Sad privilege

of priestly pronouncements, pious excessive
      for boot-to-the-cobblestone girl. Gear-shifter, word-sifter,
what destination next? What razored
      poem? At journey's end when every paper

harkens back to bark, and every word unspools
      itself unspoken, and every kiss and wound unpeels
to soon-forgotten, and every skid mark
      tapers off, here in the cage of my cold cold coffin

grief of your death is the shriek shriek shrieking
        hare in the woods, solitary pulse that inks in
the absolute darkness from my pen to my pain pain painful
        wheel steering, world stopping, time stopping, breath-stop.

The Mortician's Scar

Purely comical, his mother's leaving, her buttocks balanced
on the narrow vinyl of the bicycle seat. He nearly giggled
at the memory of the pack-mule, its burden of sacks of grain,

but that is how she zoomed right out of his life, quickly
shrinking down to a stutter through the roads he was never
allowed to explore on his own. The house was a maze of rooms,

too many to count in one afternoon, so he watered the garden
until he gutted the soil of worms. The flowerpots pissed
defiantly on the wall. And he might have emptied the land

of water, made the sleeping Sierras cough with thirst,
had his father not arrived to turn the knob. He spanked him well
into the night and it was good to blame his father's hand for the pain.

If only it had bruised his mother's cheek with whiskey, tugged
at the black weed of her braid, or even wandered through
the softer-scented alleys of the street. His mother's absence

was the puzzle that his father's presence couldn't explain.
What does the moon mean without his mother? Just another
empty mouth in the world. What is *he*? Pity that dissolves

on the neighbor's tongue like salt. Where is his father?
His father turns in bed and reaches out to occupy the second pillow,
pinches his own penis until he can't forget the hard touch

of every night that came before. But he, a boy six years away
from playing man, no matter how long he fondles it's always
that same briny odor. He shoves the taste of it, the sting of it,

Mami's midnight suckler memory of it to his own hot mouth and...
faults himself for having lost what once must have been so sugar
sweet, so pleasing to his mother. But no matter where she's gone

she took with her what's rightly his—the bicycle, his getaway
gift from Papi the week after the dogs ran rabid. The bite on his calf,
the painful shots, the scar that twitches to the ghost of russet fangs

was worth a bicycle that could outrun the fastest mutt.
And Mami learned to drive it first. She spun around the block,
then two, then three, then promised that the next time she would

come for him. *So you just wait, my son, just wait for me.*
I'll be right back, my little man, my secret on two pigeon-toed
feet, my crippled warrior, victim of the brown bitch.

The Mortician's Mother-in-Law Says Goodbye

At 70 you're still capable of the grief that wipes
its tears away with both fists. The sadness of little girls
never grew old in your eyes or in your throat—how it

hiccups rehearsing the same melancholy sounds.
Sorrow, you have learned, is two-fingered: V-shaped,
it shuts your daughter's eyelids; adjoined, it blesses

forehead, heart, shoulders, lips. Your granddaughter chased
another child around her mother's coffin and the loose
ribbon on her waist made you cry because the white bow

it once was was your creation and what a brief life it had.
The scissors, seamstress, that cut the shrouds of many,
lay cold as a pair of bovine nostrils widening against

barbed wire. You saw the cow freeze to death that winter,
and when she died she died standing, stubborn to the end
that old hide, drawn to your window by that flickering lamp—

a discard from your son-in-law's parlor.
Perhaps she had the power of the third eye, mesmerized
by the ghostly shadows of the blue hands drawn to the warmth

like moths. When the dead hold the light they
realize it is what is not them and they begin to love
the darkness that is. Old woman, you surprise yourself

tracing the last touch of your daughter's hand. It was here,
on your left breast. An awkward place, but it was not
the first time it had felt her grasp. When she suckled

as an infant it was there she reached for first, the warm milk
leaking from the raw button of your nipple. The ache
comes back to haunt you and you push it off discreetly

with your elbow. You wonder if this is how the body
begins to die, remembering its courtship of contact
and desire, moving memory back to the first sensation.

Then your daughter is here inside of you now, pressed
against the pink walls of your uterus. Slowly she
escapes you, unpeeling foot, skull and spinal cord—

you're feeling clawed, stomach turned, insides shredded.
And just as you're about to scream, your daughter disappears
completely, collapsed into the small implosion of your phantom egg.

Blizzard

Gallup, New Mexico

The heavy snow disrobes the landscape of its mountains.
I stretch a hand out the window to capture its pleasure
but it eludes my grasp because it wasn't meant for me.
Nobody knows I exist in the white month of February

and in the hungriest of hours—so ravenous they eat sound.
If there was a road it has coiled like a sleeping snake
beneath the shrinking metal of the car. I'm just as numb
in the back seat, no longer a driver, I recall that stranded

couple who survived one week on saltine crackers and body
heat. Mine is a tube of toothpaste in my bag and a man
in town who thanks me for opening my left nipple like a rose
at the prompting of his lips. When he turns his back to me

in bed his skin shades to gray and I know about the dead
who roll their eyes up to memorize the texture of their graves.
If I should freeze to death the muted explosion of my heart
will not betray me. The science of the weather will have

its own sad story to tell when I am found, ten-fingered
fetus with a full set of teeth locked to the knucklebone.
The trapped air will surrender when the door splits open
and a woman in a passing truck will romanticize my end.

Did I escape or was I abandoned? Either way I take no

possessions with me, unless I open my mouth and name
my tongue a possession. A slippery wedge of muscle, it
shifts like solid stone in the arctic of my jaw. The word

that swam to my throat, that word, *love*, grows thick
with ice like everything that keeps me company tonight:
my lung at sub-zero, my empty heart—those pieces of the body
that cannot thaw but shatter at the touch of heat.

Unpeopled Eden

2013

The Soldier of Mictlán

Once upon a time there was a soldier
who marched to Mictlán in his soldier
boots and every step was a soldier
step and every breath was a soldier
word. Do you know what this soldier
said? I'd like a piece of bread for my soldier
hand. I'd like a slice of cheese for my soldier
nose. And I'd like a woman for my soldier
heart. The mayor of Mictlán saluted the soldier
and bowed his head as he told the soldier:
We have no bread, oh honorable soldier,
we hold empty hands instead. Dear soldier,
let us take yours if we may. And the soldier
held out his hand to be taken. Oh brave soldier,
said the mayor, cheese is your soldier
wish, but we have none since the other soldier
left. We whiff empty hands instead. The soldier
let the mayor sniff the scent of his soldier
palm. And forgive us, oh strong soldier,
said the mayor, but no woman worthy of soldier
warmth lives in our empty town. Will your soldier
eyes teach us wonder and kindness and soldier
love instead? Silence stiffened the soldier
face as a search ensued in the soldier
head for a moment one moment of soldier
bliss. But all was dead. The longer the soldier
looked the more the streets of his soldier

mind resembled the streets that his soldier

feet had taken him to: where no lost soldier

finds bread or cheese or a woman to be a soldier

wife. This was no space for a soldier

life indeed. So off to the hills the soldier

fled to seek out the place where a soldier

sheds the rattle that beckons the soldier

to death to soldier to death to soldier.

Mortui Vivos Docent

I

In the trunk, a blouse with breasts, a skirt
stretched open by hips that have shaken off
the last whiff of talcum powder at the pothole.
Clumsy dancer, dropping her shoe somewhere between
Mexicali and Calexico. If she were breathing
she'd let the whiskey tell the tale,
sultry syllable after sultry syllable—sí, mi amor.
Mummies are this century's mermaids,
rattling songs that will stop a heart. If we let them,
says the whale-eyed sailor, hands cuffed
to the steering wheel, mumbling the madness
of a man who found a woman whistling
beneath a Mexican moon—music so pretty
he just had to keep it from ruining the terrorist world.

II

This is how you ruin the terrorist world:
cut out the yellow heart of heaven,
drop the bloodless stars into the sea,
blind the women who sit to wonder on the shore.
I knew such a woman. I've kept her comb in my purse
after all these years, since the night my father found her
walking home from the Cachanilla hills.
You know the names, El Abanico, El Dollar, La Puta Eva
y El Pinche Adán, places so plump with pleasure
even the air turns to stupor, drunk with a sensory coma.
Clarification: she was not the body in the ruby corset,
not behind the pair of tassels, not inside the scent
of tangerines. My mother was the mop and the bucket
wiping off the fingerprints on the promiscuous wall.

III

This is how you press against the promiscuous wall:

drill the pair of diamonds on your back and moan;

hold your breath, float face-down on the vertical pool;

sway with the shadows set in motion by a swinging

chandelier—an angry father come to claim his child.

He did not catch me then, but he caught me

walking home, my knees still numb from dancing

with the men who love their mamacitas pink

and puckered as if they're sipping wine transparent

as the cloth across their thighs. What could I do

with lips like mine but kiss or whistle loud enough

to be the visible woman my overworked mother

never was? So, papi, keep your only son holy as you stuff

me in the trunk: I'm wearing Mother's blouse, my mother's skirt.

La Pelona as Birdwoman

Tonight
I dared to crawl
beneath the sheets

to be nailed down
around me,
waiting for my lover, she

who enters
without knocking, she
who will unstitch

my every seam
along my thigh,
my side, my armpit.

She who carves
a heart out of the heart
and drops it

down her throat.
Sweet surrender this
slow death in sleep

as I dream
the lovemaking
is autopsy. How else

will I be hers
completely? Be her
treasure box I said:

a trove of pearls
and stones, the ding
of coins cascading

through her fingers.
The bird over her shoulder
not a parrot, but an owl

to be my mirror
when I close my eyes
and shape a moon-white

bowl out of my face
where she can wash
the hooks of her caress.

Still with water, I'm
one more thing to penetrate.
I'm one more spill

of secrets on the floor.
A puddle glowing green—
she doesn't have to be a sleuth

to see I've taken
all the anti-freeze.
A puddle thick with red—

she'll kneel
next to my wounds
and pray for me,

a string of pigeon skulls
her rosary.
By dawn our bone pièta

breaks out of its shadow,
unleashes its cicada cry.
My daughters drag

their bodies, bruised as bats,
out to the light
and burst into flames

like marigolds.
The crows will leap
down from the trees

to pick them clean.
And my beloved bride,
beloved wife, will laugh

until it hurts her teeth.
It's the feather
of her tongue—

eleventh finger—
I recall
and not the catheter

while the priest recites
his holy dribble
and the churchyard

worker takes a leak.
My sons hold up
their chins with pride

that they have done
their part to hide
my suicide:

they've clipped
my fingertips
to lose the track

back to my prints.
But my beloved knows:
she crouches

on the highest branch
and drops an egg
that cracks my coffin

Concussion light
squirms through
and I'm in heaven once again—

those times
we screwed like hen
and rooster: I

the squawking chicken
blacking out, and she
the hammering cock.

In the Village of Missing Fathers

Children run without shoes
because no bottles have been
broken there and no one knows how
to climb a tree or fly a kite. When the sheets
wave on the line they chirp and sing
and so no reason for feral birds.
No reason for clouds or sky.

When it rains the women never say
it's coming down, they point to the ground
and say it came. No angels hover
because no one wants flight
or things that float without water.
Newspaper boats on the puddle
are the only mystery: they refuse

to sink despite the heavy dream
of travel. They remain mute despite
the casing of words and the memory
of the grief the women poured onto the page
wishing to divine their sons' and husbands'
fates. Each article an obituary, each word
dressed for burial, each page an insult

even to the blue canaries that refuse
to plop their droppings there. And so
in the village of missing fathers

paper sorrow folds into a boat,
a bed into a holding cell for moans
that bleed out of sleep, a house thins out
into a ghost with the smell of Sunday

cologne, with the texture of a scratch
on the arm, with the sound of a throat
ringing after the triumph of carnal
pleasure. And the women watch their children
smear their laughter like paste on
any surface, hoping that something
worth keeping will stick. What wonder,

this collection of objects plucked and kept
in an empty matchbox: a leaf that sprung
out of rock, a bug constricted
in the pellet of a goat, a lock of black hair
tied with red ribbon rescued from the kindling
bucket. And the boys gather around at dusk
to fantasize about its origin: a beauty from

some other village, no doubt, perhaps
a dancer who can point to the ceiling
with her toe while standing on the other
foot, perhaps a princess who wears silver
to bed and who sips tea made from flakes
of gold, perhaps a lady whose gown
cascades with light, whose hands only need

the strength to lift an ivory comb.
But certainly not any woman from here,
the village of missing fathers, where women
have traded their silks for meats, their kisses
for bolts on the doors, the curves
of their hips for a place to carve out
the names of the dead. The boys have caught

glimpses of such scarred tissue, and it
shamed them into never watching anyone else's
mother disrobe again. Not while they soak
their bony bodies in the bath and rise
one shade darker. Not while they slip
from one black cloak into another,
the momentary flash of flesh a sad

accident, like a foot falling on
the only daisy left standing after the cow
stampede. And certainly never at night
while their mothers lie in the hollow
of the mattress and roll their torsos
in the final trace of musk that must have
overwhelmed them once, when they were

wives. Oh delicious weight of passion,
oh terrible tickle, oh precious probe.
The women are becoming brittle without it.
The boys are growing anxious with it.

The walls of every house are threatening
to collapse from the negligence of it.
But no, beloved ones, never worry,

the sad architecture of abandonment
will always stand. The broken world
spins this way: a woman runs afraid
out to the street at midnight and the moon
stops her by stepping on her braid
and all the other women come to clothe her
with shadow. The town priestess prays for her

until the woman understands that muscle
crushed to bone will take the place of touch.
And the woman hardens her resolve.
And the woman snaps her body like a jigsaw
piece back into the hole she made
when she tore out of her home, just another
wound to mend, just another

episode of melancholia mentioned over
chamomile, forgotten by the time
the tea cups freeze to yawns inside
the cradle of the sink. The children
tip their heads against the pillows
and look as fragile, as if their skulls
could crumble with the furious tap

of after-hour angst, when the trap
invites the rodent to a suicide, when

the needle's point trembles for its fix,
when the widow dresses hang themselves,
exhausted from the weight of stones.
If the children were awake they'd find
their mothers drifting in the air like errant

moths looking for a flower that blossoms
without light. They might even call them
beautiful if not for the oils that scurry down
their legs like piss. And if the women
were awake, they'd give each tiny lake
of blood beneath their feet a name.
But the broken world shows mercy

and each morning every person rises
none the wiser. The boys, fingering
their pockets stuffed with marbles, catch
the fleeting scent of something—pudenda
if they had the word, but they haven't
had it, so they run out to the road
to draw a circle on the dirt, a hole

dug in the center, an inverted nipple.
They play their game, pretending
that the aches inside their throats
are not their voices getting thicker.
If they begin to sound like grown-ups
they begin to die. That's life
in the village without handsome

men: suddenly they wear the shoes
that lose their way. Some say
they journey North to waste
their days as kitchen slaves. Some say
they trade their organs for quick pay,
and that their shame means begging
on the city streets for gauze or cotton,

stitches or thread, to heal their surgeries
and stand upright again without
rattling like coins inside a cup.
And some believe they're seized
by soldier's fury and off they run to war
on foreign lands so dry the wind sucks out
the fluids in their faces. If they regret

their choice they cannot spit. And if they
yearn for what they left behind
they cannot cry. And if they scratch their cheeks
in sleep, dreaming that they're clawing
on the buttocks of their wives they cannot
bleed. Whatever path they take, whatever
headlines speak above the rumors, no one

knows for sure, though the silence
of their vanishing comes certainly. So too
succumbing to the deadness of the air.
In this village, and many others like it,
no one talks about the missing. Not a word

about the hat clinging to the only hook
in the wall, embedded question mark

not seen since—

Not a word about the pair of slippers
hibernating like two polar bears beneath
the sofa since—

Not a word about the extra chair
that sits fasting at the table losing
weight each season since—

If the picket fences stand like crosses
never mention it. If the yellow ribbons
cut the circulation off the trees
don't point it out. Find the fallen fruit
scattered like land mines on the ground
and eat it before it explodes, before
it betrays widow and orphan with its truth:

the men are never ever coming home.

Unpeopled Eden: After the Immigration Raid

Beneath one apple tree the fruit
lies flung like the beads from
a rosary with the broken string.
Another tree stands amused
over the strangeness of a shoe
that pretends to be an apple
in its redness, though it'll never be
an apple with that lace stem
and a pit where a core should be.

The tree at the end of the row
will weep over the pillage
all week. Around its trunk, debris:
straw hats, handkerchief, a basket
going hungry for what's out
of reach. Somewhere in the orchard
a screech goes weaker by the hour.
A radio without paws, it cannot claw
its chords to end its suffering.

But silence comes, eventually,
and the apple trees will rest,
gathering the shadows to their roots
as the flame inside each apple
falls asleep. All the while, finches
perch among the branches—patient
vultures waiting for the fruit to rot.

For a wasp, intoxicated by the sugars,
this is the perfect place to nest.

The colony will thrive inside
decay: the apples softening until
their wrinkled skins begin to sink,
the seeds poking through like teeth.
The trees will sway without the wind
because the ground will boil
with larvae. A bird will feast
until it chokes and ants will march
into the belly through the beak.

Music Man

Oh father, oh music man
with a whistle instead of a coin
to toss on your walks,
keep these things for us
until we're ready to come home:

our baby teeth, fragments of bone
that rattle in a domino box.
Tuck it in your pocket but please
don't gamble it away
the way you lost our

christening gowns in poker.
We had outgrown them, true,
but what other proof
did we have that all seven
of our outfits could be stacked

and shuffled like a deck
of cards. Keep the bottle cap
opener hanging by a string.
Wear it like a locket
and stay collared to our after-school

bliss when we found you
underneath a tree that scattered
glass fruit around your feet.

The boys lined them up
for death by slingshot,

and the girls giggled
when the bodies shattered.
Take good care of our drawings,
our crooked handwriting
exercises, the scribbles of our names,

and sew a suit with sailboats
on the sleeves, a coat with Qs
sliding down a wire, and pants
that celebrate our prepubescent
autographs. And in your shoe

don't tell us which! let us guess!—
save the coin you told us
came from China. It had a hole
in the middle because the merchants
slid their change on chopsticks.

We pictured them on market
Sundays holding up their earnings
like a shish kabob. We know
you hid the coin because all seven
of us wanted it and so you

took it with you. Or so I claimed.
Can I be blamed, oh father, oh story
man, for wanting to possess

the single thing that couldn't be shared?
You saw me slide it out

the window of your wallet
while you napped and didn't
snap into attention to complain.
Of all your sons and daughters
it is I who wanted to escape the most,

to anywhere. I learned the desperate
alchemy of flowering a barren day
with song from you, oh master.
A minstrel needs his freedom.
And so you let me take it.

Gila

It's no curse
        dragging my belly across
                the steaming sand all day.
      I'm as thick as a callus
            that has shorn off its leg.

If you find me I can explain
        the trail made by a single limb.

            I am not a ghost.
Do not be afraid.

Though there are ghosts here—
        they strip down to wind
            or slump against rock to evaporate.

        Sometimes I crawl beneath the shedding,
backing up into the flesh pit for shade.
        Praise the final moisture of the mouth, its crown
            of teeth that sparkles with silver or gold.

I make a throne of the body
        until it begins to decay.

           And then I'll toss the frock—
death by hunger, death by heat—
        off the pimples of my skin.

Don't you dare come into my kingdom,
peasant, without paying respect on your knees!

What generous act did I commit
in my previous life, that I should be
                    rewarded with this paradise:

a garden in which every tree that takes root here
            drops its fruit eye-level to me.

The Bordercrosser's Pillowbook

things that shine in the night

Fulgencio's silver crown—when he snores

the moon, coin of Judas, glaring

at the smaller metals we call stars

my buckle

the tips of my boots

the stones in my kidneys

an earring

a tear on the cheek

the forked paths of a zipper

the blade of the pocketknife triggering open

the blade of the pocketknife seducing the orange

the blade of the pocketknife salivating

the blade of the pocketknife

the word México

the word migra

things that are afraid to move when they sleep

the owls carved on rock

Fulgencio

me

things that forget their shapes

snakes

our bedding

our clothes

the shadows twitching by the fire

the skin of the rabbit—its flesh

an apple

the orange

the jacaranda behind the house

the roof   the clothesline   the curtains

the door that swells in the heat

the pipes that shrink in the cold

the couch—the table—the lamp

the dominoes

the dishes

the children—the wife—the neighbors

memory

things that make noises at dawn

the sun as it rips away from the horizon
the sun as it pounds against my skin
the sand moaning with my weight
my weight moaning with the sand
the stones in my kidneys
children waking up in the homes we left behind
the footfalls—the footprints—the foot
Fulgencio's prayer without saints—or God

things that open like flowers in daylight

Fulgencio's eyes
Fulgencio's mouth—as he yawns
the buttons on his shirt
the orange peel—the campsite—the desert—the world
the jacaranda behind the house
the roof—the clothesline—the curtains
the door that swells in the heat
the pipes that shrink in the cold
the couch—the table—the lamp
the dominoes
the dishes
the children—the wife   the neighbors
memory
the white sparks in my brain
the red sparks in my heart
the stones in my kidneys

things that travel at the speed of silence

air
sand
heat
light
grief
memory
thought
Fulgencio
me

things I would say to Fulgencio if I could say them

erase our shadows

carve our names in stone

let us watch for comets while we rest

let us not make wishes that will not come true

your shoes abandoned you the way I never will

let me fan the fires on your toes

these are the final drops of my fear—drink them

these are the final drops of my fever—drink them

these are the final drops of my love—drink them

hold me—I have a flame on my tongue

hold me—you are a mouth of water

hold me   we taste of tangerines

hold me

things I want to polish clean

an apple—and another one—and another
my buckle
the tips of my boots
Fulgencio's forehead
our tracks on the sand
the ring on my finger
the horizon—its infestation of green cars
the word wetback
the voice—the bullhorn—the officer
Fulgencio's tears of shame—the sores on his toes
the sound of static—of running motors—of running men
the jacaranda behind the house
the roof—the clothesline—the curtains
the door that swells in the heat
the pipes that shrink in the cold
the couch—the table—the lamp
the dominoes
the dishes
the children—the wife—the neighbors
memory
the stones in my kidneys
the stones in my kidneys
I'd set them in gold—
I'd set them in gold—try to wear them like teeth

In the Village of Missing Sons

The old do not call themselves old;
they call themselves dead. They call
themselves forgotten and silent, the footprints
made by water that evaporate and erase,
leaving the ground thirsty for contact
all over again. They call themselves
banished, abandoned, invisible—

the winter that welcomes no guests
though it pleads for them, clearing
wide paths on streets that grow white as
bone grieving its decomposed flesh.
A wooden bench rots in the park
without a story to tell. A leg bends at the knee
without a church. And off in the distance

a body melts into the light like the final
whisper from the dying man's mouth: oh sheets,
give me more glorious buttercups that bleed.
Oh crow, morning's ubiquitous beggar,
ask me for a piece of bread, please,
please, please. Oh wall with a clock
for a mole, I'll never again turn away

from the sight of your three bristly hairs.
But no one hears such supplications
or notices the weakest of the weak wearing

moths instead of buttons, knots of yarn
instead of throats, and screwing bottle caps
into their sockets to keep the milky eyes
from leaking out. There's already a woman

haunting the streets with white feathers
on her head, and when she cries the tears
harden on her cheeks like chicken shit.
She gave birth to a son who broke like an egg
beneath a military heel, and what a surprise
to find out, after all these years, she was a hen.
She perches on a shoe at night and pretends

it's an umbilical cord and not a lace.
What a disgrace to flaunt her childlessness
that way, complain the mothers who must scratch
around the pictures of their decorated dead—
oh rosary of baby teeth, oh bellybutton crucifix—
in private. The fathers cluster at the bar to coat
their battle scars with gin. One cradles a bottle

of wine and tickles its label with his finger,
while another tries to coax the cork into its neck.
In the corner three shadows rock side to side,
murmuring a lullaby, and the bartender nods off
into dream because, at fifty-five, he's the youngest
in the village and sits closer to the memory
of infancy than anyone. He'll climb atop your lap

if it will make you chuckle, he'll let you
share your kisses with a slice of pie, he'll
even—but only for the price of a potato—let you
watch him suck his thumb. No one judges him
when he slips into his truck pajamas and begins to nest.
In the village of missing sons there are sadder
scenes than that: the mayor scolding the mice

for eating sugar and refusing to brush
their teeth; the schoolteacher reading a fable
to a row of coffee cups to usher them to sleep;
the doctor's wife pinching her nipple numb
over the orchid when it's time to feed.
In every yard tricycles rise like gravestones,
and in the fall the festival of raking leaves—

an annual archeological dig for a marble,
a miniature wheel, or the plastic head of a doll—
any toy at all that will prove that boys
once inhabited the land. One day a couple found
a slingshot, and for a week they were crowned
with the most coveted of artifacts: birthday
party hats, sun-bleached and slightly bent on top,

still celebrated symbols of the times of laughter.
But before the couple gave them back, he shot her
from behind, then shot himself, their blood
sprinkled on the frosting of uneaten cake.

No one wore the party hats again and the people
cursed the suicides for taking that away.
And curse the war with its appetite

for adolescent hearts that still contract
at the sight of partial nudity. Curse the men
who wrap their flags around their eyes to bind
themselves to loyalty. Curse the women
who allow their sons to murder other women's
sons and call it victory. And on this village
of the stupid and the blind this curse:

May you never know the magic of a child
who can point and pierce a cloud, who can
squint and cage the parakeet before it flees the house,
who can bite into a cherry and roll the world
inside his mouth, who can color in the autumn's brown,
who can pinch the sun between two fingers
and then, with childish mercy, let it out.

May the miniatures inside your memories—
little socks, little shoes, little belts and little
gloves—pop like seeds and disperse into the wind.
May the shrills of giggling, the shrieks of tantrums
sink into the smiles of hoof prints filling up
with mud. May the bite marks on your arms,
around the edges of the pastries, lose their baby teeth

and rot as you yourselves decay each childless day
in the village of missing sons. May you
call yourselves extinct and collapse among
the cribs turned rib cages, among the sticky tar pits
that used to be the swimming pools. May your shadows
vanish from the center outward and then roam
their final hours as the outlines of neglect

in the village without a playground or a school,
in the village where you drape your sagging skins
across the windows for a last encounter
with the fading light, in the village where bodies
and buildings marry into rubble and can't even
birth the dust, in the village without headstones,
without history, without names and without ghosts.

Casa

I am not your mother, I will not be moved
by the grief or gratitude of men
who weep like orphans at my door.
I am not a church. I do not answer
prayers but I never turn them down.

Come in and kneel or sit or stand,
the burden of your weight won't lessen
no matter the length of your admission.
Tell me anything you want, I have to listen
but don't expect me to respond

when you tell me you have lost your job
or that your wife has found another love
or that your children took their laughter
to another town. You feel alone and empty?
Color me surprised! I didn't notice they were gone.

Despite the row of faces pinned like medals
to my walls, I didn't earn them.
The scratches on the wood are not my scars.
If there's a smell of spices in the air
blame the trickery of kitchens

or your sad addiction to the yesterdays
that never keep no matter how much you believe
they will. I am not a time capsule.

I do not value pithy things like locks
of hair and milk teeth and ticket stubs

and promise rings—mere particles
of dust I'd blow out to the street if I could
sneeze. Take your high school jersey
and your woman's wedding dress away
from me. Sentimental hoarding bothers me.

So off with you, old couch that cries
in coins as it gets dragged out to the porch.
Farewell, cold bed that breaks its bones
in protest to eviction or foreclosure or
whatever launched this grim parade

of exits. I am not a pet. I do not feel
abandonment. Sometimes I don't even see you
come or go or stay behind. My windows
are your eyes not mine. If you should die
inside me I'll leave it up to you to tell

the neighbors. Shut the heaters off
I do not fear the cold. I'm not the one
who shrinks into the corner of the floor
because whatever made you think
this was a home with warmth isn't here

to sweet-talk anymore. Don't look at me
that way, I'm not to blame. I granted
nothing to the immigrant or exile

that I didn't give a bordercrosser or a native
born. I am not a prize or a wish come true.

I am not a fairytale castle. Though I
used to be, in some distant land inhabited
by dreamers now extinct. Who knows
what happened there? In any case, good
riddance, grotesque fantasy and mirth.

So long, wall-to-wall disguise in vulgar
suede and chintz. Take care, you fool,
and don't forget that I am just a house,
a structure without soul for those whose
patron saints are longing and despair.

Our Lady
of the Crossword

2015

Anaberto Facetimes with His Mother

He sits in Manhattan, she stands
in Michoacán, in the kitchen he abandoned
every day of his youth. How sluggish
her cooking, her hand always heavy on

the salt. Each pot a story running out
of breath long before the finish. He hides
his palates from her—behind him a table
like a gem display: croquettes of steaming

amber, rubies over salad, a string
of onion pearls flung into the omelet.
His prowess in the culinary arts
a desire he fulfills one thousand

meals apart from his beloved mother,
who inadvertently conspired to dull his senses.
Nonetheless he loves her, won't offend her
by admitting to the craft he practices

in New York—joy denied in México.
How thin my son without my stews, she fears,
how lonely and neglected he must feel
without a woman in this place he shares

with another boy, another orphan
from God-knows-where. "How is he, anyway?"

she asks, and then a second face appears,
pretty and golden as her son's. The young

man smiles, a coy expression that suggests
he isn't going hungry either. He seems quite
content in the country that her son had
fled to, she suspected, for God-knows-what.

Our Lady of the Crossword

I want to be the lady
posing naked in the nicho
of my father's crossword.

In a temple of black and white
tiles she's the only page
of beauty in México's tragic

tabloids, her smile blessed
with the serenity of saints,
her thigh coned like the chalice

of a lily, breasts plump
as cherubs and modest black stars
over the little angel noses.

No wonder my father keeps
the puzzle sacred and never
dares defile it with graffiti.

This encounter soothes him,
like a kiss of light, a yellow
bird perched on dry brush.

I want my body to bring
such a flame to his face.
I want my wink to sing.

But my father's not amused
when I shake the painted
spurs over my nipples

as I shuffle with my penis
tucked into my legs,
my baby pubes shy as nuns.

¡Ay! the wrath of lightning
strikes me down—
the tabloid pages face

the darker windows
on which my mother cracks
her hands against the glass,

helpless witness to
assault. It's not her fault.
And how to blame

my father for miraculous
conversion: his lip a smear
of prayer, a rosary whip, Our

Lady of the Crossword
tattooed like a flash burn
to the tunic of my back.

Alfonso: A Love Story

I make believe the water is blue and not this brown, polluted liquid that stinks of grease and decay, that suffocates the skin with a coat of sticky film. As I sit on the shore of our troubled little town on the Gulf of Mexico, I try to imagine it as it was seen once by the eyes of our ancestors, the fishermen who congratulated themselves for thriving in a place that would feed their children and their children's children and so on, a legacy of nourishment in every canoe, every net. I close my eyes and forget about our hunger. I hold my breath and pray that the filth will settle on the ocean floor, never to be stirred into rage again.

But this fantasy doesn't last. Always the betrayal of the wind. In the breeze, the taste of smoke, not the taste of salt, though I keep my mouth opened toward the sea and not toward the factories, their noisy metal bodies hunched behind me like exhausted creatures from some distant world. They have journeyed from so far away just to tell us the same terrible news each hour: the land is dead, the water is dead, the people are slowly dying, a death that began the moment some crooked politician with crooked teeth sold our town to the outsiders. Our fishermen have lost something great. And so have I.

I make believe that you return from the depths of the ocean on two feet like a biblical miracle. My beloved Alfonso, the champion swimmer of the entire eastern coast, defeated by the waste because we live in a place that rejects the purity of anything—air, earth, water, and love.

I sit on the shore of our troubled little town on the Gulf of Mexico as I resurrect your skin. I imagine you must have been born by moonlight to carry such iridescence, that your pregnant mother must have swallowed a pearl in the oyster, back in the days when such cravings were still possible. In the sea you were like the dolphin, playful and quick and joyous. In the bedroom you were more like a marlin, clumsy and rigid and—dare I say it? will you forgive my mischief?—spasmodic, like a fish bouncing on the deck of a fisherman's boat.

Once you worried about us getting older, about the town no longer tolerating the capricious romance of our youth. "Our sleepovers are numbered," you said, and my body grew clammy because I knew the truth of that declaration would come back to haunt me for the rest of my days.

In our troubled little town on the Gulf of Mexico, one young man's affection for another young man was just another tragedy. How we worried our mothers because we hadn't married. How we frightened our fathers because our laughter on the beach seemed so out of touch with the reality of our losses: no more fishing, no more wading, no more searching for the most intact seashell or fishbone or seaweed. Our task was to collect the broken litter: plastic bags like traumatized jellyfish, spidery threads like octopi starved to wiry membranes.

"What do you suppose this is?" I asked you once as I held out a transparent tube. You took it from my hands and began to pantomime your list: "A galactic periscope, a high-tech kazoo, a robot's ear canal." You handed it back to me. "The soul of a rose, my darling."

I pocketed the tube, which was against the rules. All refuse had to be buried at the foot of the mountain like secret stillborn. At night, your mother clutches a rosary to plead for your salvation. At night, I clutch the soul of the rose and keep your love for me sacred. I sit on the shore of our troubled little town on the Gulf of Mexico, and I try to erase that morning you washed up, just another piece of lifeless flotsam. How no one stopped me from throwing myself on the sand and leaving an imprint of my grief—a fish flailing toward its last breath. When they took your body to your mother's hut I stayed behind because I knew you were still at sea, my beloved dolphin boy, my beloved marlin man.

"We need another diver," the fat outsider from the factory said, as if you could be so easily replaced. If the town's best swimmer could succumb to the toxic waters, anyone else going down to check the clogged sewage pipes would certainly perish. Someone eventually took that risk and we expect his body to return to us any day now. The townspeople are angry and there is talk of an uprising, but emotions will recede like the tide and they will go back to being the troubled little town on the Gulf of Mexico with a beach that is no longer theirs. I know about such surrender.

And so I simply sit and wait, the self-designated watchman on the ugly fringe of the beautiful sea, imagining heaven as it is for you, as it will be for me.

My First Male-to-Male Kiss

was on Mexican TV. In the 8os. Believe me.
Like my cousin Mari, I too wished I could be
Érika Buenfil, her blonde locks so close to
René with his dark pompadour looking like a cliff
where so many broken hearts took their final leap.
Equis-eh-tú he always yelled at the start of his show
and when he pointed at the camera his finger
perforated the screen because he was choosing *me*—
me + René Casados—such last name foreshadowing—
me + René = Married, holding hands down the street
where my cousin Mari could see us and for once,
dear God, let it be *her* envious of *me* and not me
watching her stroll with the baker's son, who
fed her sugary morsels under doorways at dusk
and left me wondering what such nibbling tasted like
and could I find the crumbs collecting at their feet.
How I slipped into the black dress of her shadow,
how I mouthed my cousin's mouth and swallowed
the ghost of her sweetheart's hand whole.

I knew about pretend. I could lip-synch
to Rocío Dúrcal, Dulce and Ana Martín—*Yo te quiero,*
yo te quiero, por un beso tuyo puedo enloquecer.
I had been crooning along every week that summer
when René Casados emceed that competition
in which a voice and a memory for lyrics was all
any Mexican kid needed to compete. How else that girl

with her little arms, how else that chubby boy, face as
Indigenous as mine, how else that tall girl whose left
eye was fixed to the mic, right eye to the grand prize—
a bike that could launch its rider into neighborhoods
more elegant than the ones we lived in. I became
each contestant. Including that dainty boy with a
nightingale throat, his pixie cut exotic, his androgyny
hypnotic. It seduced the jury, audience, the bodies
in our living rooms, and even René, who rewarded
the winner with a kiss. How shocked was México
as the TV stud pressed his lips to the pretty cheek.
Yet what relief that such affection wasn't make-believe.

Bodies of Little Dead Children (1949)

after the painting by Forrest Bess

inside of me, I who will never be
a father to any he is my son or she
is my daughter or that's my baby
mirror glaring its crooked teeth back
at me.

　　　　Yet I must know something
about parenting. At night my torso
splits apart, a cradle for my heart
to pound and tantrum to delirium.

Dare I wish the little thing had
never been? Dare I ignore it,
let its cry shrink to a squeak that I
can place over my tongue?
This squirming pill bug, dare I
ingest it?

　　　　Oh cashew in the sack,
interrupted dream my barren sister
had—the pitter-pat of baby feet
vanishing like sweat on the tile
turned steam. Oh vacant nest.

Will she resent the way I squander
my fertility? Bless the tumbleweed

that chases after rain all summer
yet only flowers in a fire.

Oh lover-thief, if you steal my seeds
it doesn't matter. You're taking
nothing personal away—I will not
call the removal of my dead
a loss.

      I will not name them, either.
Where there never was a father
there never was a child. If not
a birth, then not a love. If not
conception, not a thought.
If not a wish or possibility, if not
a miracle, then not.

      Let my Calvary be this:
to fade without a trace like all
that chromosome and protein
laid to waste across the sheets.
Let my flesh go just as white
and just as cold without a soul.

Set my little children free but let
the ghosting not define me—
not a father, not a dad, yet
still alive and still a man.

Two Widowers from Aguascalientes

Not so strange, not so strange at all this
queer arrangement between two hidrocálidos
who lost their wives. Neighbors, pues'n,
guava farmers both. Don Artemio's mustache
matches the seagull silhouette of hair
connecting Don Lucho's collarbones. Of course,

none of us had ever seen their spouses
when they were supposedly alive.
Gossips claim the graves are empty,
though some swear the men have cried
before those crosses, and others say
that's where they buried their beloved horses—

a stallion and a strawberry roan that,
like their masters, never trotted out
alone. Who could blame the men for
grieving such losses? If the priest
did not object to holy burial, well,
pray your outrage at the renovated apse.

La chingada thing would have collapsed
atop the altar boys without the guava
funds by now! On Saturdays the men
ride side by side on the guava truck.
Don Lucho takes the wheel. Don
Artemio tips his leather Stetson, pues'n.

The load of guavas in the back blows
kisses from the road. Señoritas swear by them
and tempt their lovers with the pussy pink
inside the nugget. Nuns grind the seeds
and stir the powder into milk to induce
erotic dreams. What do I think? Na'a!

I just pluck the fruit off the trees. Save a few
to make my pulque—a real working man's drink.
I don't judge and I don't say, even if I
catch a glimpse of Don Artemio feeding
guava slices to Don Lucho. Men without
wives still long for tenderness in their lives.

The lesson in Aguascalientes'n, is that heart's
the center in everything—the guava, the mouth
that bites it, the palm of a man's hand wiping juice
off another man's chin. Call it sin; I'd call it Eden,
it if hadn't lasted, this paradise made complete when
two widowers pushed their empty beds together.

The Book of Ruin

2019

Parable

There's a man who sits on the shore every morning,
staring at the sea. And the sea stares back, defiantly.
It won't release its secrets. *I'll give you an answer*
if I take what you're offering me, says the sea.

When the man begins to weep, the sea yawns
with indifference. Tears are abundant here. As are
sinking ships and broken hearts and moons that drop
like shards of shattered windows. Prayers crumble,

brittle against the Caribbean wind. *There's nothing*
in your skies or on your land I haven't swallowed.
Or spat right back. The man, defeated, rises, drags
his shadow—a shadow? Or piece of cloth, a flag?

The sea keeps reaching for a closer look. The figure
blurs into the landscape and takes his story with him.
Waves crash against the rocks as if that sudden exit
hadn't left the ocean waters floundering in wonder.

What was that? The question turns to driftwood
and knocks against the mass of land, thereafter
unanswered because the man never comes back.
And so the sea sifts through its rubble once again

and again and again and again and again in order to
complete this puzzle—narratives left unfinished toss
inside memory forever. That's why the sea comes
to the shore each morning looking for a man.

El Coyote and the Furies on the Day of the Dead

where the Third World grates against the first and bleeds

—GLORIA ANZALDÚA

The car overheats as you drive
through the Arizona desert at night.
You don't panic. You coast to the side
of the road. Above you, starlight
and not much else. The moon hides
behind the mountain, gets sliced
open when it tries to climb
over the crest. The spill is bright
and reaches the trees nearby,
Their shadows stretch like
the arms of those who died
of thirst here. You can't belie
this truth: you help them die—
the promises you make are lies,
coyote. They wait, you don't arrive.
The crooked lawyer paid your fine,
the sheriff shrugged. Justice denied
the dead who gather here tonight
to hound you, a curse goodbye
before they sink back into the dry
surface of the sand. You remain inside
the car but still hear the winds chime
out your crimes, coyote. The cries
of the wronged shatter glass, pry
you from your den. Your hackles rise

in distress as you realize
you grew paws, a tail. Your eyes
yellow and balloon with fright.
You're fucked. In your hasty flight
you leave a trail of warm scat behind.
A spectral steam fades into sky.

Tsunami

There's a man who sits on the shore every morning,
staring at the sea. He doesn't have any sons
left. They dispersed like a pool of fish when the sinker
strikes the surface of the water. The eldest took

the family boat, the middle son the net, the youngest
claimed the rods, the lines, and hooks, stripping
their father of his fisherman's estate though
he wasn't dead yet. His burden was a stroke

that left him trapped inside a body—a tackle box
that lost its key. A mermaid chewed on the tips
of her hair like seaweed before scampering up
the sand just to fling a mussel shell against

his skull. He didn't move. But inside he felt elated
that for once an object came toward him
instead of floating away like everything his wife
had brought him: kisses, kitchens, sons, the scent

of jasmine on her hands and feet. She dragged
into the tide their home—no, the entire street,
the village—uprooting lampposts and eucalyptus
trees now obscene with earthworms, their moistness

desperate at the separation from the soil.
His fingers had twitched just so as he reached

for his beloved who sank into the sea, the landscape
the train of a gown that swirled down after her.

Everybody drowned, oh figurehead of tragedy,
oh ravenous water god that snatches the air out
of every lung. After centuries of villagers taking
from your belly, you had to claim it all back—

each hard-won catch, each gasp from a child
whose first fish changes color in the bucket,
each bone stuck to the throat and every story
that followed. But your wrath hungered for

more than that: each blessing over the soup,
each time a man touched his bride beneath
the table during prayer, each time a man caressed
another man in the dark, every blush born of such

affection, and every encounter with pleasure
that ended with a mouth savoring its secret
into daylight. *Give it to me,* said the sea, *every
glimpse of your woman's nipple as she fed*

*each of your sons, every bristle of your lover's
beard found on the pillow and which you fondled
while the dawn peeked through the blinds. Every
ray of light. Every time you heard the coffee*

boiling on the stove and thought What a lucky
man am I. I have everything. I have it all.

No, you arrogant fool, I have it all—your
yesterday, the days before and the days ahead.

I swallow every minute you sit there begging
to get something back. I pick my teeth with
your disappointment. Some might think it
cruel that I let you live, you the one without

a voice, but what use is a voice when no one
heeds the warnings. Your kind gave me such
taste for waste that it became addiction,
and like any dog or snake I gave in to my rage

when you weren't paying attention, when you
stood above me like a master and gazed
at the horizon as if you owned as far as
your eyes could reach. And I barked and I

hissed and told you that I too could play
that game but you wouldn't listen. What?
Is that a tear I see? Is it plump with shame
or regret? I'll savor it just the same. You,

sinking into the ruins is the story. You,
unheard is your fate. And mine. Now you know
what it's like to be me. You can whisper, scream,
it's pointless—nobody gives a fucking shit.

Corrido de la Poquianchi Jesusa*

Señores, este es el corrido
de la Poquianchi Jesusa,
era mujer rete-trucha,
no importa lo que se haya dicho—
que le decían La Medusa
pero eso es puro ruido.

Ella nació entre los pobres
en el campo de Jalisco,
Madre quería puros hijos—
machos por trabajadores;
Padre se puso abusivo
pues Dios mandó cuatro errores.

Jesusa fugó de su pueblo
rumbo para Guanajuato,
pero en muy corto plazo
las otras tres la siguieron
pues ya tenía entre sus manos
hombre, negocio, y dinero.

Delfina juntaba pupilas,
Luisa la hacía de cajera,
Carmen cuidaba las mesas,
¡vean que exitosa cantina!
Jesusa era orgullo de jefa
con su casona de citas.

Llegaron los años sesenta
seguían las hermanas a engaños
a vírgenes secuestrando
sin que los padres supieran.
Les aseguraban trabajo
pero les daban condena.

El antro con más y más fama,
el pueblo tenía sus sospechas.
Jesusa decía que por viejas
les resentían tanta lana—
gente detras de las quejas
no ganan pan con la cama.

Problemas, querían evitarlas,
cerraron el bar en apuras,
se esconden con las prostitutas,
pronto fueron encontradas.
De rapto, extorción, y tortura,
Poquianchis quedaron culpadas.

Carmen ya había fallecido,
Luisa se dijo inocente,
A Delfina la cayó en la frente
una tina llena de ladrillo,
a Jesusa le tocó la suerte
de tener que cumplir su castigo.

Las revistas decían tantas cosas,
la tele prendía puro cuento,

más gusto le daba por dentro
a Jesusa que se vio famosa,
y así conquistó al carcelero,
la sacó y la hizo su esposa.

Y así concluye el corrido
de la Poquianchi Jesusa,
era mujer rete-trucha,
no importa lo que se haya dicho—
que le decían La Medusa,
¿verdad que no tiene sentido?

---

* On the spot translation: Gentlemen, this is the ballad of Jesusa la Poquianchi, who was a very smart woman, no matter what you've heard. That they called her Medusa is nothing more than noise. She was born among the poor in the rural state of Jalisco. Her mother wanted males, men to have hard workers; her father became abusive after God sent them four mistakes. Jesusa fled the town toward the state of Guanajuato but in a very short time her sisters followed, once she had in her hands a man, a business, and money. Delfina recruited the whores, Luisa was the cashier, Carmen took care of the tables, they built a successful cantina! Jesusa was the proud owner of a very popular brothel. The 1960s arrived and the women kept using deceit to kidnap virgins without their parents finding out. They promised them jobs but then sentenced them to a life in prison. The bar became more and more well-known but the town had its suspicions. Jesusa claimed that because they were women, people resented their earnings. Those behind the complaints didn't know how to make money in bed. They wanted to avoid any problems, so they rushed to shut down the bar. They hid with the prostitutes but were quickly found out. Las Poquianchis were accused of kidnapping, blackmail, and torture. Carmen had died by now, Luisa was found not guilty, Delfina met her end crushed beneath a bucket of bricks. Only Jesusa had the bad luck of serving out her sentence. Magazines made many false claims, the TV spun its tales, but it gave her a thrill since Jesusa became quite famous. And that's how she courted the jailer, who took her home and made her his wife. This concludes the ballad of Jesusa la Poquianchi, who was a very smart woman, no matter what you've heard. They called her Medusa but that doesn't make any sense, does it?

Hagiography of Brother Fire and Sister Smoke

1. Brother Fire

Feed me. Feeeed me. These are not
the only words it knows but they're
the only words it needs. And most times,
it's two words too many. Most times,

it's coaxed awake easily and on instinct
grinds the air between its teeth. Wild
creature, a stomach in a coat of quills that
chews through anything within its reach.

Was it the caveman who first discovered
its potential—weapon or tool? Was it
the caveman who first found out it could
possibly be tamed? The others saw a fireball

careening down the hill, the creature fastened
like a second skin, a screech so singular
because this pain was new though it would be
an affliction a second body suffered through

before the sun set again. Oh miserable
addiction to destruction, to the voyeuristic
impulse to witness mass flower and wilt
into a shadow of itself. Oh dark ghost.

Prometheus was a fool to trust
the mortals who squander ingenuity
on ammunition. Even the man who
first held the wooden flute eventually

beat his neighbor with it, or so the story
goes. And when his instrument sang
out of tune he fed it to the creature who,
mad with insatiable hunger, ate the musician

too. The neighbor raised a bowl of water
to his lips and smiled as only the wicked
do. The gods looked over at the Titan
with his liver gouged and thought:

What pity to waste such a gift on
the petty, how tragic this magic turned
curse. When he figured out how to burn
things to the ground out of spite, revenge

or the sheer perverse pleasure of causing
harm, that's when the human and this
monstrosity became inseparable. Thus
the history of fire became the history of man.

Man, imperious and arrogant, named it
to claim it, to deceive himself into
believing it was under his command.
Incinerator, he called it, Purifier, Blaze,

Consumer of Detritus and Waste. But
this creature answered to many other
names as well: Arson, Napalm, Immolation,
Fire Bomb, Dragon Breath, though in the end

its purpose was the same: to feed.
Feeed me, it begs, and its keeper complies
with cornfield, sugar cane, mesquite.
The more it eats, the more it craves,

mirroring its master's appetite so
greedy its hunger is mostly whim and
indulgence. *Feeeed me*, it whines, though
if the human ear could listen it would hear

Neeeed me. Need me, as in, *The want
is all you, you belly aching baby, you
bored glutton, you bow-legged bitch
bastard son of a shit-slinging baboon.*

*That's right: you shove everything you
hate down my goddamn throat so how
else do you expect me to fucking talk,
you overstuffed bile sausage, you bloated*

sac of bloody buffalo balls? The insult
darkens into carbon and drifts out of
earshot, just another disappearing act
for a thing never to be. Selective erasure:

refusing to remember, aiming to forget.
And that's the reason, Fire, you've become
man's favorite pet. Prized in the cage of his
black stone heart you'll never die of neglect.

2. Sister Smoke

Call me Sister Smoke, groan that rises from
the burning wound, Brother Fire's fetid afterbirth,
its stink a sting—a thorn stuck in your throat—

the more you struggle to set it free the quicker
you choke. Once I come upon you its best
to let it be. There is beauty in surrender—even

the blank-eyed fish embraces resignation in
the net and halts its flailing, locks itself into a stare
that beckons. Dare to love me just like this.

Don't let my reputation frighten you, I'm
more seduction if you will, I'm less the predator
the gossips make me out to be. My twin initiates

the kill and somehow I'm the villain. What
unbecoming accusation, what travesty.
If you really want to know my story, hear me

out instead of running from me. Come.
Get comfortable. Get closer.
Once upon a time

before I was a scavenger I was a messenger.
Before I was disgraceful I was the fateful
waving of plumes in the air, merciful signal

that warned all living things *Beware the beast*
has left its lair. Not everyone escaped its path
but plenty did and word passed down

through generations that if by chance one
caught my dance on the horizon surely
there was danger there. *Beware!* It wasn't

quite affection but attention pleased me just
the same. My warnings were never called
heroic but I felt rewarded—instant recognition.

Before infamy you could say I was famous.
How I basked in my individuality. My body
seen apart from my brother's vile identity.

But fate can be so cruel, that's the rule.
The pride of presence comes with a price to pay.
Consider the royal forest that withers its leaves

when a wave of boorish rust weathers it—
a rotting graveyard ripe for Brother Fire's
ire. Consider the arrogant elk that locked horns

with a branch. I came upon this most idyllic scene,
which lasted seconds, until my brother cooked
the animal, then stripped the tree and picked

the carcass clean. Nature's beauty is ephemeral;
I'm a natural thing, as is my twin. Yet memory
clings to aftermath longer than it does

to the calm before upheaval. When man
domesticated Brother Fire to perpetrate his evil
I became guilty by association. I became

party to the rising temperatures, the droughts
and the pollutions. I lost my role as harbinger
with the industrial age and every iron cage

became my prison. A soaring spirit held captive
becomes reactive. If I asphyxiate and suffocate
you it's because I reciprocate the deed. See?

I'm simply an entity misunderstood. I only do
what you do to me. Since I'm no longer free,
the cloud of me becomes a shroud for you.

Apocalipsixtlán: New Beginning

There's a woman who squats on the sand
    the color of midnight, we don't dare call it
ash. Instead, we marvel at how midnight
    comes and the woman appears to float
like a boat. Her white tunic a sail blowing
    with the hot winds from the north, where
it is rumored water still flows. We know
    about boats, we broke them down to bones—
a mercy killing. Since they wailed the loudest
    in the drought they had to be the first to go.

We tossed the priests into the fire pit next
    for filling us with false hope. And then
the politicians for telling us their lies. They
    told the truth finally but much too late to
change our minds about burning them alive.
    We tossed the teachers and the scholars
inside the barren wells, then dropped their
    wretched books on top of them and watched
the pages swell with piss and sweat. Steam
    hissed as they cooked beneath the bubbling

paper. We heard them boil and blister day
    and night until their bodies softened into mush
and then hardened once again like plaster—
    a pool turned frieze with jaws and fingers
jutting out. Those who held such wisdom

and refused to use it were the guiltiest of all,
and thus they earned the cruelest penance:
    to melt into the pulp of what they prized
the most—worthless words, incompetent ideas.
    Despite our better judgment, we let the poet

live though with his mouth sewn shut. He
    alone keeps the story of our insurrection. Each
night before we sleep we whisper in his ear
    our precious secrets and stick a pin into his flesh
to keep them safe in case we die. If we awake we
    repossess what's ours by pulling all the needles out.
His eyes dart left and right in panic during
    visitations. We scurry down the dunes on fire
like a colony of scorpions. We are legion. We are
    condemnation—promised land turned purgatory.

Dispatches from the Broken World

New Poems

Things I Find in Abuela's Bathroom Closet

A green towel

A blue towel

Both with loose threads like spaghetti strings
I cut them off once but by the next week they'd grown out like weeds
Abuela darns Abuelo's socks and says, Just let them be

A white towel with a hotel logo

It's the nicest towel she has, though she doesn't remember
          who brought it home

A purple washcloth, its corners stained black

Shoe polish, though Abuelo doesn't have shoes that need polishing

The polish smells of gloved gentlemen in black and white movies,
          their shoes as shiny as their top hats
Do they polish the hats as well?
Abuela says, Their mustaches too
How they dance like long pencils on the ballroom floor

A box of batteries, big candle-thick batteries—for flashlights, I suppose

A wig

A very strange wig, like a dead crow on the road

I put it on and it itches when I spin it on my head
Abuela says, Don't play with that
And I say, Please, at least until Abuelo gets home
Abuela says, Just don't you tell anyone
I grab Abuela's flowered bathrobe and pretend to walk past
       those gentlemen in their shiny hats, how I blush when they
       tip them and lean in to whisper pretty things in my ear
       that sound like Pepé Le Pew—amour!
My wig comes alive like a cat and purrs
Abuela says, Silly boy

A box of bobby pins

A box of incense

A box of matches

A box of soap, the lavender I breathe when I press against Abuela

A tube of red lipstick

I have never seen Abuela wear makeup, her brown lips
       so sun-chapped from working in the fields since the '60s

A blue tin of moisturizer

A red tin of cream that smells like rancid mayo

Abuela says, Don't touch that, it burns
And burn it does, my fingers catch fire and I scream
Abuela shakes her head as she washes my hands
She wipes them clean with the green towel
I glare at the tin that reads Belly Jelly Burner Cream
Abuela says, Who knows who left it there?
She goes back to her needle and thread
I go back to the closet

A black bra like two funny hats sewn together

A black bra like a split open coconut

I'm about to ask Abuela about the black bra
            when Abuelo's truck pulls up
Abuela says, Quick, put everything away
I shove the boxes in
I push the towels in
I hide the wig and the polish
But when I stick my arm inside the cubbyhole I feel yet another box

A box I missed the first time

A box deep inside the closet's belly

A box with a plastic penis

A plastic penis like a flashlight

A plastic penis with the big fat batteries

A plastic penis with a knob I can turn

A plastic penis that buzzes but won't light up

I hold it to my chest and it hums to me
It's what those ladies in the black and white movies must feel
       when their gentlemen press their mischievous mustaches
       against their lady hearts—bird courting bird

The Storms of Michoacán

The gray wool blanket
that cushions the saddle
on the donkey.

That's what
the clouds look like
as they unfold across the sky.

And then the rumble—
collision of bulls. The hail,
coin-spill echoing

down the corrugated
roof. The sound drowns
out my mother's groans

as she twists
beneath the sheets.
I have seen such anguish

in the eyes
of the cow as her
stomach churned toward birth.

My mother's foot juts out
and trembles
as if in rhythm to

the cascade of ice
tap-tapping down
the stone steps.

I hop up
those steps—left foot,
right, until I reach the top,

where Abuela keeps
the chickens, Abuelo the goat,
and my mother her fear

of dying. How
she cried into the pens
while feeding the animals

that would outlive her,
though they too
are destined to die.

The chickens, beheaded,
will sate the mourners
at the wake. The goat

will get sick, its fever
burning the hairs off
its hide. Poor thing,

people will say,
succumbed to the family's
grief. I watched

my mother's body
grow thin, transparent
and still

in the thunder
light. Like the shirts
on the clothesline

after the rain and wind
subside. The clouds
recede behind

the mountains.
A pool of tears
collects beneath

the wet clothes.
Sorry, so sorry they
couldn't wave goodbye.

The Enchanted

The day your mother died
you were prone on the floor, crying
over some silly thing or other.

To hide from further teasing by your
aunts, you lied close to the bed,
its blanket a curtain between you

and the footsteps on the hallway
as they passed by the room, searching.
"Where are you? Where are

you?" Though they knew where
you were—you, a pill bug rolled up
into a ball of feelings. You, a boy

on the cusp of puberty, a voice
so girlish you feared to speak
on the streets of Michoacán.

The men did a double-take
and were unafraid to say, "I thought
it was a female talking!" But they

used the word "hembra," a word so
far from the word "varón," which
is what you were told you were,

therefore, act like it. You didn't know
your mother had died the moment
you stroked the blanket, the hem

on a skirt of a lady or a royal.
And why couldn't it be you
swinging as you descend

a staircase, a fan held demurely
against your face. Why couldn't—
and that's when it happened.

A silence came over the house.
No footsteps, no voices, not even
the barking on the roof. The water

boiling in the kitchen froze. The radio
stopped and sat on the sill with its
mouth wide open. The whole town

playing a game of los encantados,
and nothing can move until
someone sneaks up from behind

and pushes it into motion again.
That power was yours. You realized it
much too late because the town

lost its patience and set itself ticking
again. Except for your mother.
She, slumped over Abuela's knees

in the car en route to the hospital.
Abuela tried to shake her awake
but Abuela didn't have the magic

touch, the fairy's wand that was
your enchanting hand. *Ping!* And
butterflies flutter in the wind.

Ping! And the small black
beetle with thorny legs clutches
your finger and becomes a ring.

Ping! And your mother's name
on the palm of your hand turns
to water that escapes your grasp.

Lady, lady, scurry back to your
chamber. The hearse has stopped
at the entrance, the footmen

look sullen as donkeys with all
the weight of the world on their
backs. Open the window. Wave

your fan until you take wing.
Become unreachable, soar so high
you don't have to listen to anything.

Cicadas

The palo verde in the yard comes alive again,
spilling every secret I whispered in my mother's ear:
how I had a crush on the blonde boy in overalls;
how I stole a deck of cards from Zody's but never
used them. The chimpanzee on each card judging me
with eyes that refused to blink. I told my mother this
and many other things though she wasn't really there
but buried in an old cemetery a country away, where
the spirits flew in each November on the orange wings
of monarchs. Since we have no butterfly migration
in Southern California, cicadas will do, their song
not a song exactly, but a scream at the sun, the heat,
the bright yellow flowers of the palo verde—at all summer
fires that remind me that life must go on despite
my grief. *Tell everyone about me!* I yell at the tree
as I rummage through the branches for exoskeletons.
The cicadas can never be caught. But I punish them
for their brief lives by crushing all evidence of their
existence between angry forefinger and sad thumb.

Family Reunions

Each September is the anniversary of my mother's death, but she doesn't visit as often as she used to. I sense her presence though, much like the feeling I get when I think I've left the door unlocked or the stove on after taking the first step onto the street. My father died one October, many decades after my mother. He has not been gone long enough to forget his way back to me. He brings with him rooms I haven't entered since childhood and insists on seeing me as a boy, though I was in my thirties when I said goodbye. Perhaps because I was only a teen when *he* said goodbye to me, he'll always remember me that way, walking to school with a backpack over my shoulder, so innocent to his plan: moving out while I fiddled with a protractor in math. We perform the same play each time we meet in my sleep: I pretend I'll never know what abandonment feels like and he makes believe that he's been waiting for me all this time. My cousin Verónica visits often. She wears her little girl body when she takes me by the hand. She'll stand next to me or sit next to me, but she never faces me. She looks out at the horizon for the arrival of her sons. Only her eyes betray the terrible truth she hides inside her younger self: that her boys can never exit the orphanage in which they've lived since her death. What unique cruelty in dreams, where the anxieties of the dead merge with the traumas of the living. Although I never loved him and I'm certain that he never loved me, I'll take Abuelo any night instead. He appears undisguised and unconcerned, coming back to claim what was only his: the kitchen, the living room couch, and the large TV. He notices me eventually, and asks me to step aside, or go outside, or he simply pushes me away. I don't belong here in the hurts of the past. But his rejection is not an act of mercy or kindness. It's an act of returning to what was so familiar to both of us: my absence from his line of sight, his distance from my need to comfort the lonely child in me.

Xoloitzcuintin

after Rufino Tamayo's *Animals* (1941)

Or, in my grandmother's tongue, uíchu-echa.
Or does it matter? The bite is just as cruel.
I would know. I stood safely behind the gate
with the family dogs at my side. Pepe, so
hairy and loud. Pina, so small but vicious.
When the boys who pestered me at school
walked by, I threatened to let the dogs out.

The boys laughed at my sudden courage.
Me, flanked by these nervous animals
whom I had not seen attack anyone.
Not even my uncle, the man who stuffed
their puppies in a sack. The log struck-
struck. And then the night grew quiet
without the whimpering. Pepe and Pina

became even angrier after that, barking
at passersby with such force, my mother
was certain that one of these days the dogs
would lunge from the roof and tear a body
apart. I began to imagine canine teeth
sinking into flesh. A fountain of blood
and a fountain of tears, cartoonish yet

horrifying, like Ojo Canica's fake eye.
How at birthday parties he would grant

a boy's wish and place the eye on top
of his slice of cake. The children cackled
while the old man looked sullen, resigned
to the truth that this was the only reason
he was ever invited. Oh, the aches of my

childhood. Here is how to fill a dog
with pain—by clobbering its heart; here
is how to pluck a man's dignity and
pretend it's all in fun. And here is how
to tell the boy who made me touch
him that I like him too: with the hook
of my finger, I open the gate's latch.

To the Boy Who Was Night

after *The Small Boy Who Was Night* (2016), a painting by Tino Rodriguez

I too used to place a veil over my head.
I was either a widow or a bride because
they both left something behind at church

like I had on the day of my first communion.
How I envied the girls in their white
gowns. The lace of baby cribs that kept out

the flies made me feel so otherworldly,
angel-like. But I was taken to the altar
unadorned and stripped of my crown.

Standing next to a girl in silk gloves,
her Cinderella slippers poking out
like doves beneath her dress, I felt

absent, removed from my true self.
When the priest placed the Eucharist
in my mouth, he stored a piece of bread

on an empty shelf. It remains there,
unclaimed and forgotten like that child
at the altar whose heavenly light never

reached the spot where he stood.
I want to tell you, dear one, that light
doesn't only come from above. It also

comes from within. I have felt its heat
many times: the first, when I walked
into a field of sunflowers and recognized

the beauty of my kin; and when I borrowed
Mami's lipstick to plant a ruby kiss on my
reflection; and when I draped Abuela's white

rebozo around my shoulders—how I
shuddered, shaking off the cold gaze
of ridicule from school. I learned to be

as confident as a butterfly, as elegant
as a moth: dodging shame by coming out
of hiding every day. And then each night.

Our Lady of the Wound

for Ai

The candle doesn't bleed but drinks
its wax back in at the altar of Our Lady
of the Wound. No, she doesn't want

stale prayer or eyes that plead—watery
stare so close to death it flickers like
the moth tempting fate near the flame.

Our Lady of the Wound will not
mirror your pain. Or faith. If you
approach, save your grievances

for more kindhearted saints,
those who wear their martyrdom
like afterglow, who stand at the corner

of the church like trash receptacles.
Don't you dare pin your milagros
to her gown. Don't kiss her toes

and then act surprised when she
kicks you in the mouth. Woman who
cries out when any door slams shut,

you've been told. Man who holds
his scrotum in his sleep, keep away.
You're so insipid it's vulgar when

you stand before Our Lady with no
interesting story to share. But you,
queer boy with painted nails, please

hold up the silver charms on your wrist
so she can take a closer look, not
at the bracelet but the cut beneath it.

Our Lady of the Wound would
peel it off if she could, rub it clean,
erasing every word in the tale

about a boy who lost his way
through a forest. The wolf crept in
seductively, caressed his scrawny

arm in the dark. How he pimpled
at the touch of bristles. How he
bit right through his soft lip

when those fangs pierced his skin.
Your Lady knows all about such
damage, child, and she'll keep you

company until the sun comes up,
her scythe a warning to the wolf.
Our Lady of the Wound is watching

now. Our Lady of the Wound will
keep your secret sacred as a rosary
and hold it tight around her finger-

bones. When she bares her skull
through the black hood of her robe
she's showing you she welcomes

you, her kin. Underneath your
frock of scars and bruises you are
solid rock. As impervious as she.

My College Boyfriend Asks
Me Why I Kiss with My Eyes Open

I tell him, Because my last boyfriend took
my wallet, and wink. I tell him, Because I want you
to stay. If I stop looking at you, you might
sneak out of the room. If I keep my gaze

fixed to your body, I can glue it
to mine. Wherever you move I'll follow.
He says, That's creepy. Co-dependency
isn't sexy. I tell him I'm only kidding but he

leaves me anyway, one limb at a time.
The last night he kisses me he too opens
his eyes, which are as green as clover,
my lucky charms. Or so I used to say until

I saw them up close, so full of fury like those
velociraptors in the movies that keep still
until they rush in for the kill. And then I wanted
him gone, lanky legs and arms heavy as logs that

pinned me to the bed. I dreamed that he died
atop me and I had to fight my way out. What's
worser than worse? the comedian in the dorms
asks. A truckload of corpses. What's worser

than that? You, at the bottom of the pile.
What's worser than that? The only way
to freedom is to cannibalize. Forget it.
Goodbye, Velociraptor Eyes, you and your

predator's hunger. The next boyfriend
also asks me why I keep my eyes open
when I kiss. I tell him that when I was young
the neighbor's son came to visit. He closed

the bedroom door and stuck his tongue in
my mouth without warning as a kind of joke.
I stared at the door, hoping no one broke
the spell, but just in case, I kept watch

for intruders, for the sound of shock at the sight
of the neighbor's son eating every last
drop of saliva I had saved up for this very
occasion. TV couples taste each other's

meals, cocktail drinks, and chocolates.
That's why they always order dessert. Especially
after seafood. I had been sucking on peppermint
candy cane the afternoon the neighbors

came over to drop off tamales and to pray
with my grandparents who didn't go
to church. Let the boys play, the woman
said, they're so innocent. What was

his name, that boy who entered me
with such horrible breath? I knew what Abuela
was thinking as the devout people next door
murmured until her leg fell asleep: this

better be worth the trouble. When they left,
we ate the tamales and they weren't
very good anyway. And I said, Don't let them
trick us this way again. I pressed

my buttocks to the chair to wipe off
the pain. That boy, such a nasty little jerk,
slid his fingers down my pants and poked
my anus. I froze and said to myself, You

idiot. The danger wasn't behind the door.
I tell my new boyfriend all of this.
He sighs and says, You have trust issues.
He's a psychology major and he reads

into everything, even the way I suck in
my stomach when posing for photographs.
You have body dysmorphia. And eating
disorders. You need to seek help, he says.

When he sleeps over, he snores so gently
I want to smother him with a pillow.
I stay up all night, in case he wakes up
wanting to put me out of my misery first.

Las malditas flores de tu despedida

Sobre el puente de sombra y cama
        te encontré, amada
madre mía, contando las sortijas de la muerte.

Cuatro, cinco, seis...
        ¿con cuánta plata te seduce?
Y, ¿cuántas horas me quedan para no volver a verte?

        Amada madre mía, tus manos hechos piedra
derraman terrones. Qué puñalada
        me diste, cuánto ajo lloraron mis pinches ojos,
            y qué herida me chingó la vista.

Entre el callejón de sombra y cama
        te encontré, amada
madre mía, besándole los dedos a la muerte.

Qué perra La Pelona,
        presumiendo anillos y un corazón
de monedero apretado contra la cadera.

        Hasta las arrugas de la cobija
se quedaron congeladas. Vaya, con qué sonrisas frías
        salieron a la calle, amada madre mía.
            Se quedó la puerta bien despierta,
        pero la ventana se queda muerta todavía.

Your Darling Matricide

How now to convince your killer that his father
did exist, when your only proof crumbled
like a powdery moth at the textile factory fire
sixty years ago? For nine months you carried

two precious gifts inside your apron: your only
child and the picture of your lover, age eighteen,
who vanished North. The day you gave birth,
your apron, left behind before your journey

to the midwife, succumbed to the flames. And so,
the law of God: that one face replace another.
No matter. Your lover's kiss branded on your nipple
met your baby's hungry mouth. Feeding time was how

your son would get to know his father. That and
baths by salty water on the sand, where your lover's
naked afterimage stands. But this didn't impress
him much, child called bastard, Mami's boy who

didn't have Papi to send him to the corner for more
cigarettes or beer. And so, childhood rage slicing open
cats too trusting to escape. He tossed their skulls
into the turf to bob like flotsam. When one washed

ashore one day, you wondered at that shell that looked
like a severed kitten head. When you discovered

that indeed it was, you sank into the sand as if
the weight of your child's crime was now your burden.

You should have known then that he'd grow up
to be the kind of man who would tire of his old and
useless mother, she who could be easily dispatched
by boat, just another catch thrown back into the sea.

Instead, you waved at him as he played soccer with
a group of children on the beach. His body dark and slim
like all the others. When one of them waved back
you thought *Yes, that must be him*, all childish glee

and innocence. You lose that boy this night he
rows the boat. He stares at you with cold indifference,
eyes blank as winter moons. *This can't be him*, you think,
heartless fisherman ignoring an old woman's pleas,

her anguish glassy-eyed beneath a starry sky. "What
will your father say?" you ask. "I have none," he replies.
You insist he does, blushing at the memory of that
afternoon your lover came galloping on horse

to shore, where you sat collecting clams. He said
you wouldn't get pregnant if you made love in the sea,
your pubic hair flowing like moss as he dug into your
hipbone to secure his pearl. When sleep turned sweat

to brine, your bowels twisting eels, he left your side
and a picture on your chest—a promise to come back

one day. Suddenly, you see him there inside your son—
liar, coward, trickster, thief—sorry shadow of what

could have been a man. "Goddamned beast!" you scream.
"¡Que te lleve el diablo a chingar a tu madre!" You rise
to strike but he shoves you to the black. You hear him
say before your splash, "I have no mother either."

Siento

a Francisco X. Alarcón cento

amanecí mudo y triste, sin sol
te escucho, abro las puertas, las ventanas
tu voz es un murmullo verde de oasis
una antorcha en lo oscuro del monte
me diste una canasta de manzanas
yo las adoro como relicarios
al verme en ti, descubro lo que soy
yo ya no soy el mismo, ya no soy el ciego
por las escalerillas que has subido
todos, por fin, salimos vencedores

Cómo llegar al panteón de Tzintzuntzan

Al entrar al pueblo mágico de Michoacán, pídele al taxista que te deje en frente de la iglesia de San Francisco y el Señor del Rescate. La placita está llena de puestos, pero aún cerrados. Los artesanos Purépecha llegan después del atole. Al fondo, el arco de la entrada al Atrio de los Olivos de Don Vasco de Quiroga. Ya casi no hay árboles, pero hay bastantes bancas de acero para sentarte. Descansa, hijo. Si quieres darle gracias a Dios, bienvenido al templo que ha visto pasar el tiempo desde 1538. Si quieres darle un vistazo a la historia, acércate al museo, el ex-convento de Santa Ana. No está abierto. Has llegado muy temprano, pero aún puedes olfatear la antiguedad de los muros, y escuchar el llanto de nuestros antepasados que todavía lamentan la llegada de los españoles que nos clavaron la cruz en el pecho y su lengua sobre la nuestra. Los artesanos empiezan a llegar. Consuélate al oirlos hablar Purépecha, la poesia de tu abuela. Sal a recibirlos mientras acomodan sus ollas de barro. Han llegado los colibrí, pero en pintura, o hechos de madera y palma. Si los vendedores te invitan a ver su mercancía, sé respetuoso. No sabes quién de ellos sea tu pariente. Saluda a la anciana con el rebozo azul. Tiene los mismos ojos que tu abuela y tu papá. Dile que regresas en un momento. No te cree, pero se sorprenderá cuando lo hagas. Sigue adelante, a la orilla del autopista Páztcuaro-Quiroga. A la izquierda están las yácatas tarascas. Ahí, al aire libre, es dónde oraba tu gente antes de rezar en la iglesia. Les dicen ruinas, pero bien sabemos que no se extinguieron las llamas de nuestro ser. Aquí vivimos todavía, y aquí seguimos falleciendo, pero no sin dejar huella, mapa, y decendientes. Al fin, el panteón. Fíjate qué metáfora: el cementerio dividido por el autopista, invador de asfalto. Nos apartó como camas gemelas. Ahora nos vemos con tristeza, como hermanas separadas por la frontera. El sollozo es más largo que trenza. *¡Jikeni kánekua tsïpesïnga exeni!* El grito constantemente irrumpido por el ruido de motor. Tú que tienes vida, hijo, únenos caminando de un lado al otro. Los días de muerto ya pasaron, pero nos dejaron vestidos de oro. Nuestras velas no se olvidan del fuego. Tú no te olvides de nosotros. Quítate los zapatos. Sume los dedos en la tierra. La sangre que corre entre tus venas nos llama. Los dormidos y el despierto ya juntos. Pirekua de la sombra se enlaza con pirekua de la luz. Nana Kutsï, Tata Jurhiata, *juchá pirésïngaksi, juchá pirésïngaksi.*

Afterdeath

A truck perches on the sand, exhaling its final
breath. Sunset arrives to watch it grow pale
as the desert wind twists the rosaries that cling
to the cabin's mirror. Christ collides against
Christ before either can utter their prayer.

A weary elephant, the truck has traveled
from far away to die here where others have
died before, eyes just as dry and blank.
The surrender so graceful, so peaceful
it might well be just another creature

lying down to rest after a day beneath
the heat. If it remains undisturbed it will
dissolve into the soil. Desert is compassionate
that way, granting any carcass or corpse
its burial. Until then, the truck will sleep

above ground, its temperature rising each hour,
cooling down each night. Morning again.
A curious thrasher lands on the large white body.
Its chirp so distant from grief, as if the truck
could wake, then resume its slow migration.

Desert Lily

This white dress will not be worn again, says the wind,
and the dress lets go of its fondest memory: clinging
to the clothesline as it made believe it was a kite.

How it soared, gull-like, through the sky, how it
cast a shadow independent of a body, and escaped
the human grasp like sunlight or a butterfly.

The past is a prison anyhow. As are names,
says the wind. The wind arrives not because it's called
but because it's forgotten. When it wails it mocks

the old women who cry for what they lost.
This white dress will not be mourned, says the wind,
and the dress comes alive even more. The ruffles

on the hem opening and closing like the valves
of a heart. Pebbles and sand erode from the cloth
and the white dress begins to flower once again, a

desert lily that will glow with moonlight. This white
dress, says the wind, belongs to no one. What
strange freedom this detachment from the living,

from the scrutiny of eyes that covet or desire,
from the touch and tug of human hands that value
all they can possess or possibly destroy. This dress,

this white dress, can invent its own beauty
for a change. It can dress itself. Here, a collar
made of larvae. Here, a scorpion for a buckle.

To the Boy Who Wanders toward the Border

I call him Juan, but he doesn't answer. I call him Jesús,
and then Demetrio, and then Raúl. I even offer to let him borrow
my own name, but only for the few seconds it will take him
to hear me, stop, and turn his head. He will have to give it back
once I catch up to bring him home. My name is much too long
for him anyway. Even from a distance I can tell the ends will brush
the ground. No harm done—desert dust shakes off so easily.
Artemio! I shout and the footprints on the soft sand stir awake,
but those are not the boy's. So, I bow my head apologetically
and move on. Perhaps my mistake is assuming he speaks Spanish,
so I switch to Purépecha, our mother tongue. He has to be from
Michoacán because of the black ribbon on his hat and by the coloration
of his wings. I call him Auani, which means rabbit. I call him Axuni,
which means deer. But this only pulls *my* body south and now
I'm fluttering away from him. Now I'm completely out of earshot.
The boy thins out like the matchstick succumbing to the flame
and I become nostalgic for my Tata, for how he used to hold a match
until the heat reached the callus. How he never lit another
cigarette or sang pirekuas after my brother left, my brother no
older than the boy I can't reach. Every boy going away is my
brother vanishing all over again, is Tata closing his eyes like
the lid of a coffin coming down to hold in the secrets of the dead.
The boy is not a boy anymore but the word before thirst, the word
that sinks into the sand like a button or a tooth or an eye or other
things that come loose on a trek. The boy not boy but sunset. The boy
not boy but string of smoke that wanes just before the dark end
of the wood in the firepit warns us that the world is growing cold.

Cage

Thousands of unaccompanied migrant children could be detained indefinitely

—NEWSPAPER HEADLINE, 2019

In a world of loss
    gratitude is what
       I demand for keeping
    precious catch
within my reach.
    No one despises
       the shepherd for
    collecting his flock.
No one accuses
    the watchman of
       making a captive
    of his charge.
I'm like a holster,
    or sheath, all function
       and no fury. Don't
    you worry as I
swallow you whole. Those
    ulcers in my gut
       are only windows,
    the stoma punched
into my throat is just
    a keyhole. Don't be shy.
       Hand me the rattle
    of your aching heart

and I'll cradle you,
    bird with broken wing.
        Let me love you. I
    will hold your brittle
bones together. I'll
    unclasp your beak
        so you can sing.
    Ours is a world of always
leaving but here
    you can always stay.

Bond: A Tale

after *The Bricks* (2006) by Reena Spaulings

On my way to find my father, I came across
this wall. And the wall said I couldn't pass
without formal permission. *Permission?* I balked,

then attempted to walk around it, climb over
it, and even run through it, but the wall was
too wide, too high, and too thick. Despairing,

I was ready to give up, turn around, and head
back to my little village, which felt empty
ever since my father went away. My heart

was going hollow; the last memory of my
father's embrace was fading, fading, fading.
I said to the wall, "You may be stubborn

and cruel but I will break you down, brick
by brick!" I began to sing the joyful songs
my grandmother taught me, and the wall

began to soften. I danced to the music
of my people, and the wall began to wave,
flag-like, in the wind. When we grew tired

I sat down and it rested right beside me,
draped over my shoulder. We fell asleep.
When I woke up the next morning, the wall

was stretched out, taut as before, and yards
apart from me. Stunned at the wall's betrayal,
its rejection, I began to cry and scream. I

shook my fists and cursed until I heard—
surprise!—my father's voice behind me. No
need to check. I had awakened on the other side.

Man at Desk

after the drawings of Martín Ramírez

I

There's a man who sits at his desk this evening,
bearing witness to the end of days. The more ink
he uses, the less breath left in the world. He writes
the word *bees* and the buzzing stops, all hives
explode into dust, and no one remembers honey.
Not even the man who sits at his desk, looking
down at the word as if he had just invented it.
Bees, he mutters. The awkward sound sputters out
of his mouth and plummets because it lacks wings.
The man smudges the page. The word, singed
into illegibility. He tries to recall its circular shapes,
retrace its final journey, but it's much too late
to bring back to the light what's been erased.

II

There's a man who sits at his desk this evening,
wondering what to do with this new word, *song*.
It is mute like the sparrows outside his window.
Stubborn as the kettle that no longer whistles
no matter how much the water boils. The man
at the desk rolls the word around with his tongue
but it refuses to make sound, inert as a bell.
What now? Spit it out? One more tragic tale
to shame the world? Already the flutes turned
back into wands and the saxophone into a horn
that will sleep under glass in a museum. *Sigh*.
The man tries to awaken the word one last time
by biting into it. No resurrecting the demised.

III

There's a man who sits at his desk this evening,
sick with worry. The plows have stopped plowing
farmlands stretched at the foot of the mountain.
The entire range deflates with the weight of sun.
The man regrets writing down the word *window*.
He lights a candle, cursed to continue in shadow.
Everything this square on the wall once shared
has been withdrawn: the clouds no longer there,
nor the sparks of orange butterflies now trapped
midflight as if wedged unkindly into stained glass.
He barely hears the cows and the coming storm,
so he tiptoes across the room, creaks open the door.
Nothing enters. He will have no visitors anymore.

IV

There's a man who sits at his desk this evening,

watching the word *flower* wither to nothing.

It is not yet winter, but every garden retreats.

In his, ink blots shrink down to poppy seeds

and the rose on the desk flattens its flirtatious eye

into a line, sharp as a needle. The man extends

his hand and pricks his thumb. A drop of blood

falls on the page but disappears before it blooms.

And then his quill, once majestic as pampas grass,

thins down into a vulgar stem of rye. Beauty is

small, gets smaller. Frantic to reclaim it, he sketches

petal within petal within petal until the curves stretch

into parabola inside parabola—spirals of the wretched.

V

Without *wheel* there's no escape. Without *sky*
there's only the prison of this room. The man
draws a four-legged creature and a machine
slumped on parallel lines but dares not scribble
their names. Look, there's a woman with a word
frozen on her lips. Let it remain unspoken lest
it be gone forever. Let it not be *love*. Let it not be
God. When the man rests his head on her dress,
she assures him that she will keep the word intact.
Weary of loss, he wills himself gone. He writes:
There's a man who sits at his desk this evening.
There's a man who sits at his desk.
There's a man.

Pandemic, Mon Amour

This is not the poem in tercets that I wanted.
I'm not pleased with its slanted rhymes or that title on it.
Maybe I can switch to a sestina, or better yet, a sonnet.

This is the poem I wrote while in quarantine.
Lockdown took my concentration but by day thirteen
I had mastered the oven and the washing machine.

At first, I worried about meaningless shit like will I
ever visit Greece? Without a gym how can I exercise?
I stressed about getting laid. Until my friends died.

One was a novelist, the other a poet. Their names
absorbed by data. I cried into the title pages
of their books. I pressed the dampness to my face

because I had to hold back tears for later grief.
The park across my building has begun to green.
This calming view gets shattered every time a wailing

siren lunges at the street. And once again I'm blank,
the desk flatlines right before me. I'm incapable of link-
ing words that can be legible behind the N95 mask

of the computer screen. What stupid metaphors.
I can't escape pandemic lingo or the viral sheen
that coats my poetry. I'm stuck in 2020, mon amour.
Take me back to the age of quatrains, pre-COVID-19.

St. Covid, St. Corona

We covet the birthmark dying on your face.
If we had mouths, we'd kiss it, but the gods who made us
gave us windows through which everything escapes.
The last man we held slipped out of our arms
like a fish and he took the entire canoe with him.
Let us fondle your mole like a wet papaya seed
and we'll build something bigger, beautiful and black—
an avocado with a bubble of gold instead of a testicle.
Let us love you from within, we'll change your tulips
back to the poor white roots that growl like scars.
And then the spidering commences: node crawling after node.
We'll remember you each time a monitor crickets
because its chirp is just another small thing we let go.
And though the gods who made us gave us legs
we are like chairs to weigh down your chest in place.
We travel nonetheless. When you sleep we move
into darkness; when you dream we hide among objects.
When you die we guide you through the funnels
of final song. Let us know when you're done making
a honeycomb from the ball of wax that is your heart
and we'll show you how to turn the bed inside out:
from your bones the wood, from your skin a shroud,
from your tears a dozen cherries on the ends of cigarettes.

On the Sickbed, among Crows

Agony from the light bulb as you lick your dry teeth,
          watching the crows on the wallpaper.
The crows want to pick what's left of you clean.
What remains is still yours, however: shoes that have lost not one
but both feet; a belt that no longer holds the belly up;
two nickels and a penny that missed the last pocket to the street.
On the dresser, a dying man's wallet and the useless
folds of its mouth. Your children taunt you, feigning normalcy
from the family photograph nailed to the wings
          of the restless crows on the wallpaper.
The shock in the crow eyes, dark as bullet holes, will not unfreeze.
In fact, they're as full of rage as your body, which wants
to split open and set you free. For now, you're as trapped
          as the crows stuck to the wallpaper.
Your wife is nowhere to be found. No use looking around
anymore. She melted down with the votive candles
into a puddle of fat and grief. Her replacement in a nurse's cap
is too weak to swat the crows from descending while you sleep.
The nurse has tired of dodging bird shit and wants
to remain unseen; she turns the light switch off. She's out
          in three like the crows on the wallpaper.
The dark crushes your lungs, kicking up dust you cannot swallow.
And then not a sound. Not even a cough.
Not even skid marks in the flurry of crows as they feed.

Tzopilotl (#45)

The Lost

Like our other gods, it's hungry. Unlike
our other gods, it's airborne, fugitive
bird from hell, whose red feathers have charcoaled
because it now lingers like a black star
above the certainty of our deaths. We
have traveled so far on this pilgrimage,
across mountain and desert, unable
to reach that elusive horizon that
golds in the daytime and diamonds at night.
This is the end of our journey. But this
is not the god we were searching for. This,
the god that found us when we lost our gods.
Our wails awakened it. Pleading summoned
it to our hiding spots. What did we do
to provoke its wrath? Oh mercy! We caused
neither harm nor wrong. We followed the path
to paradise and our faith came undone.

The Vulture

Humans kneel before anything they fear.

The Lost

If we close our eyes, can we cloak ourselves?

Perhaps it will pass us by, a shadow
grazing our backs so gently from above
we will call it consent to stay alive.
What if we wish it gone? Can we pray it
away? We're so many, surely there's strength
in numbers if not, then safety. We can
frighten like a tidal wave, or block like
a wall, or spread out like an oil spill
and mirror back a shadow larger than
this so-called deity, its rage so not
divine at all. What kind of god just waits
for its meal to die and cook itself in
the sun, anyway? So lazy, passive,
not so much a ferocious god. Maybe
this black feathered thing is no threat to us.
Maybe it never was. Did we really
see it fly? Does it actually exist?
What trickery, what lies deceive our eyes.
Angels and demons are not the only
creatures in flight. Wings also grow on birds,
on wretched scourge of the earth like that one
dragging its talons across sky without
effort. It glides with the wind. Let's hold
our breaths, watch it drop on rock and crack
its skull! No pity on the one who showed
no kindness to the ones who begged rescue.
We asked for a spark of hope and got none.

The Vulture

What's worth interrupting my daily flight?
Nothing. And certainly not you. Or you.

The Lost

Are gods held accountable when minions
rise to rebellion? What price will this one
pay? Let's pluck each feather out and send it
squawking in the heat until it scorches.
Let's chop it down to bite-sized pieces—let
the scavenger be scavenged for a change.
The deeper we sink into indignance
the closer we come to snapping its beak
wide open and pulling out its greedy
tongue. May it starve for love twice as fast as
we have. May its light taper down to dusk.
No silence more devastating than what
follows unanswered prayer. May you be
the supplicant whose words refuse to leave
your mouth, then tumble back into the gut
to cut you open from inside. If you
could see the world from the ground where we thirst
and bleed, you too would curse the gods who watch
you suffer from a distance. How dare they
soar when they're not our rulers anymore.
Tzopilotl, you have forsaken us.

The Vulture

If the skies are the roof of this planet's
mouth, and the land its jaw, then I'm moving
through its epic yawn, the blank boredom that
fails to catch the eye. There are days when I
surprise myself and pay attention for
just a second or two. I might even
venture down into the mud. Rare that I
visit though. The long descent is tiresome.
And for what? For these tedious humans
and the incessant squeaking of their wants?
Give me shelter, they shriek. Give me water.
Give me honey, give me light, give me life.
Give me this, give me that. Give me, give me.
Scarce grace in their asks. None in their demise.

The Lost

Tzopilotl, you have forsaken us.

The Vulture

...

Village without Souls

Every home squats without its door and gapes
like the mouth of a fish going dry on a beach
where the sea receded long ago, before
the last footprint kissed the foam goodbye
and sunk into sand like stone. Every window
lost its purpose and went blank as the eyes
of the last dog standing on a patch of grass

that died beneath its feet. It waited for direction
but thirst for anyone's affection got there first.
The dog collapsed with the weight of neglect
and now lays on the lawn like the mitten
abandoned without its twin, never to caress
or be caressed, never to be loved for the warmth
it once offered to the last living humans who left

without their belongings or pets. When the wind
rushes through the hollow structures along
the street, no one responds to whistle or
screech, to wail or howl, to any "let me
whisper my name in your ear" or any "fuck off,
I didn't love you anyhow." The only memories
spilling out are of bodies that exited each house,

their ghosts cycling through the thresholds when
the gust from the east pushes the dust off
linoleum floors and rocks crooked tables leaning

on broken legs. But not even the winds take
pity on the wounded creatures and let them
stand in misery another day. The deciduous trees
grow weary with age and stand over their own

waste as they're forced to watch everything
around them die an undignified public death:
the church trembles beneath the burden
of silence as the steeple bends in final prayer
to the end of holiness; the bell drops from
the tower like a stillborn and the stained
glass loses its color in anguish; the headstones

on the churchyard fold over the last traces
of human gesture in order to kiss the brittle
skeleton flowers and the fragile mud cups
of heel prints; a granite cross tips over
and becomes an X without meaning or
function; the churchyard gate, accepting
its fate, begins its slow descent into burial;

the statue of the Virgin Mary has lost her
hands because the faithful have forgotten
how to ask for blessings, and she how to dole
them out. Have mercy, plaster fingertips
gnawed off by rodents that once feasted on
their young. Have mercy, holy nose picked
off the face. When thunder comes at night

and lightning strikes, a pale skull flickers
like a dying beacon. Have mercy, raindrops
spitting on the robes of saints. What's pain
when the only heart that hasn't shattered
is encased in rock? What's grief when
no one heard it suffocate? That chirp
cutting through the dark is the ache

of floorboards at the altar. That bird pinned
to the wall has starved to death, waiting to
be free. But it too will be consumed by the fire
snaking through the pews. Goodbye wooden
cage that splinters and crumbles. Your sacred
bird uproots and rises in a plume of white smoke
The sky puckers up and slurps it whole.

The Trees Keep Weeping
Long after the Rain Has Ended

just as I keep moving long after my body stops
at the door. The sidewalk turns the corner and there
I go, smooth as the sailboats of Puerto Rico

that drift into quiet thought on the horizon.
The boats float over the sun's reflection, leaving it
behind to shudder on the cold surface, alone. My body

knows such abandonment whenever I'm four steps
ahead of it. Some mornings I catch the train
just before the doors close. On the platform,

my body slumps over its cane, looking betrayed
and forlorn. When the train zooms into the tunnel,
for a minute or two I deceive myself into thinking

that my body will never find me again, that I'm
free, finally free of that slowpoke who takes away
my dignity at the airport, where I'm forced to board

on a wheelchair even though I can do so on my own.
Is it really gone? Where are the NYC subway acrobats
with their loud music and peddler hats? I want to

spin around the pole with them, jutting my feet
in the air. My backflip will not be as spectacular
as theirs, but give me time, fellas, to get used

to this. I too was young, I too could dance
without affliction once, a very long time ago.
But just before I get lost in daydream entirely

I notice my body looking back at me
from the mirror of the window. Weary yet intact,
it made it to the train after all. And I'm ashamed

to have misjudged its capability. How stupid. It is I
who needs to catch up to this body, its persistence
and grace—how it makes itself so public, defying

stares and second looks, how it's unafraid to be
the center of attention, like that sailboat at sunset
that doesn't drift away as I once believed. It shows

the way. *Here, timid sun on the water*, the boat
says. *I'm clearing a path for you. Not so you can
follow; so you can travel right beside me. Let's go.*

I get it now. Just as the trees weep long after the rain
has ended, so too the heart beats while the body's
not in motion. And while it rests. And while it sleeps.

To the Man Who Walks with a Cane

Welcome back, old friend, the stairs
    didn't miss you though they've waited
        at the same spot, in the same pose,

loyal as a dog and just as patient.
    The doors are as arrogant as always
        and will refuse to step aside as you

come through. You pause on the NYC
    sidewalk. The current of bodies curves
        around yours. You, the steadfast stone

at the center of the creek. If a story
    took place at this corner between Macy's
        and Madison Square Garden, you'd be

the last one asked to tell it,
    though you are today's most reliable
        witness. There's a woman in an orange

dress who spills like yolk into the crowd.
    A double-decker bus rushes in to lap her
        up. A tall man walks hand in hand with

a 7-year-old version of himself—same
    pale legs, same baseball cap. They both
        turn when the ambulance sneaks up

behind them. They look nothing alike.
 A young man holds a pretzel as if he's
  looking at a galaxy. How lovingly he eats

star after star. When you hobble forward
 the city street is unresponsive because
  it wants you no less or no more than any

other anonymous pedestrian exchanging
 one view of the skyline for another.
  When a man with the same cane

crosses paths with you, you wonder
 if your canes recognized each other
  or if they refused to see the fleeting

truth of this encounter. You and that
 man pulled the canes and yourselves
  apart. A tear so slow and so painful

it's still hurting when you lie back
 in bed and shut your eyes. In that
  twilight before sleep, you revise

the moment of the meeting: no, you
 didn't simply pass each other by,
  you stopped mid-street and stopped

traffic too. Every person froze in place,
 as did all noise, except for you and this
  man who blink in unison. The evening

so still your eyelashes are a band of cymbals
   clapping. You keep your hands to yourself
      because eye contact is evidence enough

of human warmth in this place and time.
   Now everything's aware of the matching
      canes, their holders face to face, fusing

two stories into one great kiss that turns
   blue holding its breath until you both
      agree to let the restless world move on.

Unfathered

I'm middle-aged and bachelorhood
went to the party without me.
Not only am I my father's age, but
my grandfather's as well, though I'm

no father or grandfather to anyone.
In my 30s, a man who wanted to be
a father asked me to be his partner
in parenting, but I was so young,

so gay— fatherhood was a costume
in a play I would never want
to sit through. Daddy was the man
who paid for my drinks and whose

grey beard nuzzled my thin neck,
the stale odors of vodka and Calvin
Klein cologne stayed on the sheets
long after I'd forgotten his name.

In my 40s a woman asked me
to father her children. She also gay,
she with a dream to mother
a brood of half-Black, half-Mexican

babies I could visit any day.
And I said yes. Yes to children

leaving handprints in my living room,
yes to tiny mouths smearing yolk

on my books and milk in my bed.
Yes to the gurgles and cries too
unruly to lock up like toys in a
box. Yes to papa pretense.

I saw myself closer to the men
in my family, to their worries
and joys at having someone
else with whom to spend their

money and their time. I too
wanted someone to grieve
at my loss and to remember me
years after I died. BELOVED

FATHER, prized achievement
engraved on granite so that
even after death any passerby
would know what I bequeathed

to the broken world. Yet, babies
never came. I walked away
from cradles, baby bottles,
and the badge of honor

memorialized on my grave.
Sometimes I visit that

cemetery. A bright bouquet
of flowers—marigold, myrtle,

and baby's breath—an offering
to the father I might have been,
but also to the father I never had.
How I yearned for his approval

and affection. How I've walked
the lonely earth and will continue
walking still, mourning the men
too improbable to come true.

Hurt Bird

The cold winter imprisons
me again, my sadnesses
my only company.

But not today.
Perched on the ledge:
a pigeon missing

one leg. It stands
in place despite
the strong winds.

Its feathers part
to show its goose-bumped
flesh and the redness

of a wound.
I have a hurt bird
outside my window.

I resist a rescue
to massage its bruise.
If it drops,

ending its life,
I will be the only one
to grieve its absence.

This death will be
one more sadness
to carry into January.

If it breaks open
on the sidewalk, eight
stories down, I will keep

the unexpected joy
of its visit like balm
in my hands to rub

against my body
during lonely nights.
But I'd rather have

the bright light
of its survival. I'll pray
for a miracle from

this side of the icy
glass. And to think:
just yesterday

I had vowed
to throw myself out
the window.

Surely, I can't disturb
this creature's refuge.
Surely, I can wait.

To the Old Man Who Sits on the Horizon

Only yesterday you seemed far away.
Today you're so close I can sense your
breathing, incarnate silhouette much clearer
than the day before. Your ears as crisp

as butterflies newly sprouted from their
bone cocoons. I look back at my younger self
and marvel at everything I left behind
with him: my fear of loneliness, of aging,

of falling asleep and not finding my way
to daylight again. Abuelo mourned his teeth
more than he cried over the loss of his legs.
Gone were the kitchens of his ecstasy

and the tasty slaughter of pulsing meats.
The lineup of small spice jars stares from
a distance like headstones people have
ceased to visit. Abuela, out of pity, stuck

a piece of corn tortilla in his mouth
and Abuelo nearly choked to death,
and that was the last flavor of home
he would ever dissolve on his tongue.

Was it cruel to remember what once
had meaning? Was it more valuable now

that it was gone? By the time I take
a seat beside you, old man, I will know.

What do the dying hold in their hands?
My father kept a bottle of beer—his
loyal companion present during the births
of his children and the demise of his wife.

He perched it, like a bird, on his knee.
When the sun was about to set he let
the bird go but it had long forgotten how
to be free. It sank into the sand, becoming

the widower my father used to be,
puckered lips going dry, yearning for a kiss.
I'm in the stretch of the journey where I
get to decide what stays nestled inside

the cradle of my fingers: the book
I never finished? my wedding ring,
the only vestige of a very short marriage?
an alebrije from Oaxaca, reminder of

a paradise that scattered a trail of stars
each night to ensure her children's safe
return? Your shoulders tremble, old
man. It must feel cold to sit exposed

on the horizon where even the ocean
and the sky look flat and clenchable

as photographs. Old man, you're not
shivering, but laughing. I can't wait

to find the humor in a lifetime of sorrow.
How liberating to chuckle at the fools
behind you, slowed down by the weight
of their pasts when peace awaits just ahead.

A Note on Resentment

While traveling in México, I spent a weekend with friends of friends in Texcoco. They had a white dog. I don't recall whether he had been inherited or rescued. But I won't forget this detail: he had worked in a circus. To prove it, my hosts threw a stuffed animal into the pen and the dog seized it, running a wide circle close to the fence as if in rehearsal for a performance in the ring. But instead of simply holding the stuffed animal as he ran, he swatted it about violently, a kind of rage that seemed unbecoming of his training. "He thinks it's the monkey," my hosts told me. "He's likely traumatized from all those times he had to carry the monkey on his back. So now he's getting his revenge." My host laughed at this speculation, which seemed logical, if not a bit unfair, since the monkey too had been trained to ride the dog like a horse, likely wearing a precious hat and leather vest. The monkey too had been imprisoned by its garb, its commands, its inability to break out of an indoctrination that shrunk its knowledge of its body, agency, and place in the world. I watched and pondered: *Who am I in this equation? The dog or the monkey?* I used to be the monkey, locked inside my fear of not being liked, trapped by the need to be loved. Now I'm the dog. I'm definitely the dog. I hope to shake past burdens off, but even into middle age I'm still unwilling to let go.

The Wind Has Stopped, the Desert Listens

And yet, I have no sadder story to offer
    than the wind's. The wind just whispered
the names of the dead, but I wrote
    them down on the sand. The sand
already knows those who perished
    and doesn't want to mourn them again.

The wind, so compassionate, whisked
    those names away. Though in its
haste, it snatched my own right out
    of my mouth. My poor tongue went
numb, as if it too had been severed
    from my body. I puckered my lips

to comfort it with a kiss. I have had
    much practice over the years, soothing
it when expressing pain, calming it down
    before causing more harm. Perhaps
its stunned silence is not such a bad
    development. Not in this landscape,

which is much larger than all our
    names twitching together like a nest
of mice. If I had traveled to the sea,
    I might never have been heard. If I
had hiked up the mountain, never
    been seen. So I walked to the desert,

where any movement is an occasion
    worth noticing. For lack of speech,
I dig my feet as I step forward, but
    this solemn narrative is so familiar
that it will blend in with the dry sage
    and chaparral, the faint hint of its

survival going up in scented smoke
    in the healer's hands. When my foot
snaps a twig, I cringe as if I had
    broken bone. These are not the tales
I want to leave behind. In the desert,
    apology and complaint sound the same.

Therefore, I will tender neither.
    When my sweat makes viscid trails
on my cheeks I rub them clean. Oh
    sticky fingers, help me hold on tighter
to this glorious palo verde. Let me climb
    those gray boulders without slipping

into the void of their cold shadows.
    I know about a man who went missing
here. I didn't realize it until now,
    as I stand on rock looking around,
that I have come in search of him.
    Perhaps it was his name torn away

from me. Or rather, I cried it out
    to the air so many times, the wind

pulled it apart like a cactus flower.
    I'm so sorry, dear friend. I'm weak
and lonely. I can only think about
    myself and how I've taken your place

on this hot day. A jumpy creature stirs
    in the brush and I'm reminded of
my heart those evenings we embraced
    in bed. The curtains billowed like sails
and I became convinced, for one brief
    moment, that we were adrift, unmoored

from my family's judgments. How you
    threatened them for keeping us
apart. How your tears became
    emblazoned on my chest. They still
burn like welts and I have followed
    them here like a sailor guided home

by looking at the map of stars. Yes,
    I remember now, how my father
tossed your shoes out the window,
    how their mouths widened in shock,
how the desert received them as it
    welcomes any wanderer or castaway.

You must have suspected all along
    I wouldn't join you. You held
out your hand and I cowered, hare
    trembling in its den. Your hand

so empty and pale like the dead
       opossums on the road we pitied

and prepared for burial. When
       did you know I would betray you?
The night you asked me to stand
       naked next to you as your body
sang to the full beaver moon?
       I pretended to be sleeping, afraid

to be found with my lover—a man
       who could shatter, not with the stones
of my father's disgust, but with a touch
       withheld. Mine. My love, I let you go.
I watched you plunge into the vast
       horizon until you melted in the light.

I didn't deserve to keep anything
       that was yours. Not your caresses,
not the memory of your breath
       against my face, not even your name.
There. My task is finished. I surrender
       my story, part shame, part grief,

in exchange for forgiveness. What
       has been spoken here has gone quiet.
I'll retreat to the place for those who age
       with regret and die alone. Farewell,
my love, I have kept you my secret
       for 35 years. Today I set us both free.

Boxes of Ashes

México lindo y querido,

si muero lejos de ti,

que digan que estoy dormido

y que me traigan aquí.

—CHUCHO MONGE, 1940

1. Jorge Negrete, México's singing charro, recorded this song in 1940,

2. but it wasn't until his death in 1953 that the song became famous.

3. Negrete died in LA at the age of 42. His wish was for his lifeless

4. body to be returned to his homeland. He had recorded that wish 13

5. years prior, in that song about dying away from home, which says:

6. *Mexico, beautiful and beloved, if I die far from you, tell them I'm*

7. *only asleep and to bring me back to you.* My mother was afraid of

8. dying in the US because her family would have no access to her final

9. resting place. We traveled back to Zacapu, Michoacán because she

10. knew she was dying. She died in 1982, a few months after we

11. arrived. My mother was 31 years old. She died in a car en route to a

12. hospital in Morelia. The songwriter, Chucho Monge, was born in

13. Morelia, but is buried in Mexico City. He's buried in the cemetery

14. for notable Mexican figures, the Panteón Jardín. Negrete is also

15. buried there though he was from the state of Querétaro. Negrete's

16. actor-singer compadres, Pedro Infante and Javier Solís—collectively

17. known as Los Tres Gallos Mexicanos—are also buried there.

18. Infante died 4 years after Negrete. Infante died at age 39 while co-

19. piloting a plane that crashed in Yucatán. Solís died, 9 years after
20. Infante, from complications after gallbladder surgery. Solís, the last
21. of Los Tres Gallos Mexicanos, was 34 when he died. Panteón Jardín

22. is also the resting place of the great Spanish poet Luis Cernuda and
23. of Salvador Novo, the great Mexican writer. Both were openly gay
24. and both died in their 60s. Cernuda left Spain in 1938, at the onset

25. of the Spanish Civil War. He lived in the UK, the US, and finally
26. México, where he died in 1963. Federico García Lorca, Cernuda's
27. good friend, was killed in 1936 at the age of 38. Lorca was killed for

28. being an activist, and for being gay. Cernuda died in exile and Lorca
29. was killed at home. My father's parents died 7 years apart. Abuelo,
30. who was born in California, died there in 2004, at age 77. Abuela,

31. who was born in Michoacán, died in California in 2011, at age 82.
32. They're buried together in Coachella, a town they didn't like. Abuela
33. did not want to die in the US. She didn't want to be buried here

34. either. Abuela's dying wish was to spend her last days walking
35. through the streets of Zacapu, a goat cheese sandwich in her hand.
36. She wanted a burial in Nahuatzen, her hometown, or in Cherán, or

37. in Tzintzuntzan, where our Purépecha relatives have loved, lived,
38. and died for generations. My mother and Abuela would have known
39. "México lindo y querido," because they both loved Jorge Negrete.
40. But in our home, the anthem was "Caminos de Michoacán." This

41. song was written by Bulmaro Bermúdez, who was born in
42. Michoacán the same year as Abuela. The first man to sing it was

43. Federico Villa, who was also from Michoacán. He first sang it in
44. 1974, and is still singing it. The song is about a man returning from
45. distant lands to reconnect with his sweetheart. But she has since

46. moved on. Now he's searching for her, town by town: "Caminos de
47. Michoacán/ y pueblos que voy pasando,/ si saben en dónde está/
48. por qué me la están negando." The love story isn't what appealed to

49. my family, but the roll call: La Piedad, Pátzcuaro, Sahuayo,
50. Zitácuaro, Apatzingán, Morelia. The song also names Zamora,
51. Villa's birthplace, and Ario de Rosales, Bermúdez's hometown.

52. Michoacán towns triggered our nostalgia, and we longed even for
53. the places we only knew by name. After I turned 50, I began to
54. appreciate how important it was to choose where to die, or where

55. to be buried, if one had that choice at all. I was born in California,
56. like Abuelo, but I grew up in Zacapu. Like my mother, I want to
57. come home in the end, but not to a burial. I'll be cremated. In 2018,

58. I had my mother's remains exhumed, then moved to the church
59. crypt. Her burial place at the overcrowded Panteón San Franciscano
60. was crumbling with neglect. In the unit where her ashes are kept,

61. there's space for 3 more urns: for her parents, who are still alive,
62. and for me, her gay son. The Vatican decried cremation, until we
63. ran out of space. They approved cremation in 1963. Except ashes

64. cannot be scattered to the winds or divided among grieving
65. relatives; they have to be housed in a holy place. My father died in
66. 2006. His ashes were handed to his second wife, who kept them

67. atop the TV. I knew my father wanted his ashes scattered at el Cerro
68. del Tecolote, the prominent mountain visible from any Zacapu
69. neighborhood. He'd go hunting there on Sundays and our family

70. hiked up afterwards to eat the kill, usually squirrels, opossums, and
71. garter snakes. We didn't go to church on Sundays. After a short
72. time atop the TV, my father's ashes were scattered unceremoniously

73. behind his house in Mexicali, a border town he didn't like. My
74. mother's urn was a simple pine box with a cross and a nameplate
75. but with her maiden name. A box doesn't tell the full story of a life

76. lived, just the story of a life come to an end. By the end of summer
77. of 2020, the US had over 180,000 coronavirus deaths, which
78. included foreigners in the country, like the workers from México.

79. On July 13, the Mexican consulate of NYC presided over the re-
80. patriation ceremony of 200+ victims of COVID-19. The urns were
81. covered in black cloth, a white ribbon, and a white rose. The dead

82. were essential workers: health care providers, food service
83. employees, and custodians. 105 were from the state of Puebla.
84. There are so many Poblanos in NYC, more than from any other

85. state in México. They live here, they die here, but some don't want
86. to stay here. The 105 dead returned home, taking 105 unfinished

87. dreams with them. Burial at home no longer matters to the dead

88. but it makes all the difference to the living. Juan Gabriel, México's
89. greatest singer-songwriter died in 2016. He died in Santa Monica,
90. preparing for a concert. His ashes were returned to his adoptive

91. home, Ciudad Juárez, Chihuahua. But the people of Parácuaro,
92. Michoacán, where he was born, protested. That he was gay was only
93. discussed in public after his death. But everyone knew. And now

94. that everyone says it, nobody cares. His songs are my anthems,
95. particularly "Se me olvidó otra vez." It was recorded the same year
96. as "Caminos de Michoacán." The song opens: "Probablemente ya,/

97. de mí te has olvidado," addressing a lover who has gone away. The
98. heartbroken speaker promises to wait in the same town so that if
99. the lover returns, their reunion is certain. For me, the speaker is

100. México. I'm the unrequited love who fled to another country
101. but hopes to return, a gay man's ashes in a box, to rejoin his
102. mother/motherland. The ending: "Que nunca volverás/ que nunca

103. me quisiste/ se me olvidó otra vez/ que solo yo te quise." It has to
104. be true: no one misses me, dead or alive, like the place called home.
105. Or welcomes me back, dead or alive, like México, México, mi amor.

3000-Year-Old Poem

Writing on stone may be the oldest in the Americas
—NEWSPAPER HEADLINE, 2009

Likely Olmec, likely couplets, likely a prayer
to the maize god, or the rain spirit, or the feathered

serpent—an ancestor to the Aztec Queztalcoatl, god
of air, of wind, of learning, its opened mouth not

a threat but a missive, likely a lesson, likely a sermon.
Perhaps those words of wisdom were carved on stone

to teach or to warn those who came after the decline
of this Mesoamerican civilization about how time

sees the end of everything humans touch or hold
up to the sun. Say goodbye to the fields of corn,

to cassava and sweet potato. Say goodbye to deer,
antlers scratching sky, to peccary with hairy sneers,

to the opossum that carried away her seven sacks
of babies for cooler dens. They never came back

to the place where rivers quieted down to crusty
beds of mud that hardened like the skins of thirsty

alligators. Reptiles too dried up and died with the grass,
the reeds, and the catfish that swam among the moss.

And the rain. What happened to this blessed gift
from heaven? If the gods felt affronted, bereft

of tribute and offering, blame the fury of the land,
its blistering volcanoes whose toxic heat descended

on the soil, poisoning streams. *Our climate changed*,
declared the king, defeated, his helmet edges singed.

As the empire began to crack, its people scattered,
leaving behind colossal heads that once mattered

so much as symbols of lineage and history. Jade
bracelets, gold pendants and other heirlooms traded

for a road to other languages. The shaman deserted
his temple, the scribe abandoned his awl but alerted

future monarchs and serfs about what weather's wrath
awaits—this message: likely a poem, surely an epitaph.

Tostón

And then you open your sleepy eyes one morning
to discover that half a century has gone by.
That you left your beloved mother 38 years behind,
your father 14. You don't remember ever wearing

the white gown of virginity because someone
stole it long before you knew such a gown existed.
Yet you won't forget about the theft because, since
then, every man who touches you walks away with

something. You keep a small clay pot next to the bed
It will fit inside the space in your chest once you lose
the last chip of your heart. That's the golden rule
of the body: whatever you keep inside is breakable.

You stopped trying to glue your youth back together
because that which has shattered remains shattered,
and, besides, it's not a pretty picture anyhow.
Neither are most of the days that followed.

The saving grace is that no one's left to pressure you
to clean yourself up. You have grown and now
you're growing old. What's worth the hassle to mend
if you can't wear it again? What's the point

of regret when every eyewitness to your mistakes
has died? You stay in bed because you have no one

to feed. This doesn't bring you sorrow. The silence
in the room is neither haunting or daunting.

The floor collects the cells of your skin and no one
else's. You're breathing in only yourself in the dust.
Again, this doesn't sadden you one bit. Perhaps
you used up the last drops of grief after you lost

your children. When you die, you're the last piece
of evidence that your parents ever lived. And you?
What proof that you were once loved? Slowly
you rise and walk from one room to another

and both rooms scarcely notice the difference.
You are, dear friend, officially a tostón that 50¢
Mexican coin, half a peso, relic of the past, purveyor
of the simple pleasures of your childhood—paletita

de dulce sabor mango, canica ojo de dragón,
galletita de mantequilla, cacahuate japonés.
Moctezuma's profile is engraved on this silver
moon, he always facing away from the sea,

looking back at the ruins of Tenochtitlán, not
with anguish or disdain, but with a dignified gaze
that says, *What is done is done. No use crying
over what can never change. Or what is gone.*

ACKNOWLEDGMENTS

Many thanks: Eduardo C. Corral, who planted this idea in my head; Martha Rhodes, Ryan Murphy, and #TeamFourWayBooks, for their enthusiasm; Toi Derricotte, who gave me the best advice on how to shape the book; Gary Soto, who still has my back after all these years; and to all the editors, especially Sally Ball who worked on three of my books. Gratitude to the University of Illinois Press, Tupelo Press, and A Midsummer Night's Press for permission to reprint poems. Thanks to Fiona Chamness and Bridget Bell, for critical eyes. This labor was supported by a 2020 New Jersey Individual Artist Fellowship and a 2020 Lannan Literary Fellowship. New poems appear in *Antología poética de escritores latinoamericanos* (Fondo de Cultura Económica Perú), edited by Zyanya Mariana Mejía; *Beauty is a Verb II* (Cinco Puntos Press, 2023), edited by Michael Northern, Camisha Jones, et al.; *Big Other*; *Buzz Words: Poems About Insects* (Everyman's Library, 2021), edited by Kimiko Hahn & Harold Schechter; *The Eloquent Poem* (Persea Books, 2019), edited by Elise Paschen & Gabriel Fried; *Foglifter*; *Killer Verse: Poems of Murder and Mayhem* (Everyman's Library, 2011), edited by Harold Schechter and Kurt Brown; *Poems from Pandemia* (Cork, Ireland: Southword Editions, 2020), edited by Patrick Cotter; The Academy of American Poets Poem-A-Day Series, selected by Oliver de la Paz; *Guernica*; *The Nation*, with thanks to Kaveh Akbar; *The New York Times*, with thanks to Khadijah Queen; *Together in a Sudden Strangeness: America's Response to the Pandemic* (Knopf, 2020), edited by Alice Quinn; and *Writing the Self-Elegy: The Past is Not Disappearing Ink* (Southern Illinois University Press, 2023), edited by Kara Dorris. "Xoloitzcuintin" was commissioned by the MoMA Poetry Project, many thanks to Ada Limón for the invitation to contribute. Hugs to those who were only a text away during the pandemic, when this book was assembled: Eduardo, Erika, Sandra, Janet, Maria, Mahsa, Oliver, Rick, Kimiko, LeAnne, Natalie, Carmen, Sarah, Ura, Manuel, Rich, Pablito, Diana, Ann, Victor, Enrique, Ricardo, Michael, Reggie, Joseph, Fazlur, Max, Alice, John, Lauro, and my brother Alex. Many thanks to my community at Rutgers-Newark for making the last 15 years possible. This book is also in memory of four very special souls lost to the pandemic: Hache, Vittoria, Elvia, and Christina. And finally, with much affection, to Marx.

Rigoberto González is the author of eighteen books of poetry and prose. His awards include Lannan, Guggenheim, NEA, NYFA, and USA Rolón fellowships, the PEN/Voelcker Award, the American Book Award from the Before Columbus Foundation, the Lenore Marshall Prize from the Academy of American Poets, and the Shelley Memorial Prize from the Poetry Society of America. A critic-at-large for *The LA Times* and contributing editor for *Poets & Writers* Magazine, he is the series editor for the Camino del Sol Latinx Literary Series at the University of Arizona Press. Currently, he's Distinguished Professor of English and the director of the MFA Program in Creative Writing at Rutgers-Newark, the State University of New Jersey.

PUBLICATION OF THIS BOOK WAS MADE POSSIBLE
BY GRANTS AND DONATIONS. WE ARE ALSO GRATEFUL
TO THOSE INDIVIDUALS WHO PARTICIPATED IN
OUR BUILD A BOOK PROGRAM. THEY ARE:

Anonymous (14), Robert Abrams, Michael Ansara, Kathy
Aponick, Jean Ball, Sally Ball, Clayre Benzadón, Adrian
Blevins, Laurel Blossom, adam bohannon, Betsy Bonner,
Patricia Bottomley, Lee Briccetti, Joel Brouwer, Susan
Buttenwieser, Anthony Cappo, Paul and Brandy Carlson,
Mark Conway, Elinor Cramer, Dan and Karen Clarke, Kwame
Dawes, Michael Anna de Armas, John Del Peschio, Brian
Komei Dempster, Rosalynde Vas Dias, Patrick Donnelly,
Lynn Emanuel, Blas Falconer, Jennifer Franklin, John
Gallaher, Reginald Gibbons, Rebecca Kaiser Gibson, Dorothy
Tapper Goldman, Julia Guez, Naomi Guttman and Jonathan
Mead, Forrest Hamer, Luke Hankins, Yona Harvey, KT Herr,
Karen Hildebrand, Carlie Hoffman, Glenna Horton, Thomas
and Autumn Howard, Catherine Hoyser, Elizabeth Jackson,
Linda Susan Jackson, Jessica Jacobs and Nickole Brown, Lee
Jenkins, Elizabeth Kanell, Nancy Kassell, Maeve Kinkead,
Victoria Korth, Brett Lauer and Gretchen Scott, Howard Levy,
Owen Lewis and Susan Ennis, Margaree Little, Sara London
and Dean Albarelli, Tariq Luthun, Myra Malkin, Louise
Mathias, Victoria McCoy, Lupe Mendez, Michael and Nancy
Murphy, Kimberly Nunes, Susan Okie and Walter Weiss,
Cathy McArthur Palermo, Veronica Patterson, Jill Pearlman,
Marcia and Chris Pelletiere, Sam Perkins, Susan Peters and
Morgan Driscoll, Maya Pindyck, Megan Pinto, Kevin Prufer,
Martha Rhodes, Paula Rhodes, Louise Riemer, Peter and Jill

Schireson, Rob Schlegel, Yoana Setzer, Soraya Shalforoosh, Mary Slechta, Diane Souvaine, Barbara Spark, Catherine Stearns, Jacob Strautmann, Yerra Sugarman, Arthur Sze and Carol Moldaw, Marjorie and Lew Tesser, Dorothy Thomas, Rushi Vyas, Martha Webster and Robert Fuentes, Rachel Weintraub and Allston James, Abigail Wender, D. Wolff, Monica Youn